T0369623

The Battle Against Poverty

The Battle Against Poverty

Colombia: A Case of Leadership

Juan Manuel Santos

Former President of Colombia
Winner of the Nobel Peace Prize 2016

OXFORD
UNIVERSITY PRESS

Great Clarendon Street, Oxford, OX2 6DP,
United Kingdom

Oxford University Press is a department of the University of Oxford.
It furthers the University's objective of excellence in research, scholarship,
and education by publishing worldwide. Oxford is a registered trade mark of
Oxford University Press in the UK and in certain other countries

© Juan Manuel Santos 2023

Translated into English from its original Spanish version by Lisa Taylor

The moral rights of the author have been asserted

All rights reserved. No part of this publication may be reproduced, stored in
a retrieval system, or transmitted, in any form or by any means, without the
prior permission in writing of Oxford University Press, or as expressly permitted
by law, by licence or under terms agreed with the appropriate reprographics
rights organization. Enquiries concerning reproduction outside the scope of the
above should be sent to the Rights Department, Oxford University Press, at the
address above

You must not circulate this work in any other form
and you must impose this same condition on any acquirer

Published in the United States of America by Oxford University Press
198 Madison Avenue, New York, NY 10016, United States of America

British Library Cataloguing in Publication Data

Data available

Library of Congress Control Number: 2022951463

ISBN 978-0-19-288523-4

DOI: 10.1093/oso/9780192885234.001.0001

Printed and bound in the UK by
Clays Ltd, Elcograf S.p.A.

Links to third party websites are provided by Oxford in good faith and
for information only. Oxford disclaims any responsibility for the materials
contained in any third party website referenced in this work.

Acknowledgments

I want to express my gratitude to my family and the people who supported me in envisioning and developing this book.

My eternal gratitude goes to my former professor, Amartya Sen, who promoted the theory of human development and inspired the Multidimensional Measurement of Poverty. This book is, in large part, a tribute to his valuable contribution to humanity.

I also extend my special thanks to Sabina Alkire, co-creator of the Alkire–Foster method of measuring multidimensional poverty and co-founder and current director of the Oxford Poverty and Human Development Initiative (OPHI), who was instrumental in this project's development and who helped refresh my memory and review the book; to John Hammock, co-founder of OPHI, for his enriching dialogue; and to Felipe Roa-Clavijo, who, first as the coordinator of the global Multidimensional Poverty Peer Network and later as an associate researcher at OPHI, also supported reviewing the text, provided valuable advice during the writing process, and played an essential role in obtaining the complete bibliography that is cited as a reference.

Additionally, I want to acknowledge Diego Zavaleta and Roberto Angulo, who participated in the process of building the Multidimensional Poverty Index for Colombia (C-MPI), whose interviews and articles were extremely useful; and María Lorena Gutiérrez, who, as one of my closest government advisors, worked on establishing and implementing the Poverty Roundtable and dashboard and who helped complement my memories.

My gratitude goes also, and in a very special way, to Juan Carlos Torres, who was the director of speech writing in my administration, for his dedication to this book's preparation, research, and coordination: without his support, the book would not be a reality; to Natalia Roa, my very diligent assistant and the communications director at Fundación Compaz, for her logistical support; and to Lisa Taylor, who, as a translator, rendered this text originally written in Spanish into good English.

Finally, of course, I deeply thank the millions of Colombians who, between 2010 and 2018, overcame poverty or improved their living conditions. Just as the victims of the war, with their fortitude and generosity, gave me fuel to fight "the battle for peace," the most vulnerable Colombians were those who motivated me to fight another, no less important battle: "the battle against poverty." And I fought it side by side with a great government team and the best of armies: a social army composed of thousands of Red Unidos (United Network) caseworkers who, against all odds, supported the families most in need on their path to overcoming poverty.

Not only do I thank them and all those who get up every day and go out to build a more just and equitable Colombia and world, but I also dedicate this book to them.

Letter to the Reader

In the second decade of the twenty-first century, Colombia saw encouraging and somewhat surprising results in the fight against poverty. While the percentage of Colombian people in poverty (according to their income) was 40.3% in 2009, this percentage fell to 27.0% in 2018.[1] In the same period, extreme poverty (again measured by income) decreased from 14.4% to 7.2%.[2] This means that more than five million Colombians—more than one-tenth of the country's population—overcame income poverty and that the number of people in extreme poverty fell by half, all in less than ten years. Multidimensional poverty measurements confirm this progress: while in 2010, 29.7% of Colombians were poor according to the Colombian Multidimensional Poverty Index (C-MPI), this percentage was reduced to 19.1% in 2018[3]—a difference of more than ten percentage points.

What actions were taken in Colombia to achieve this progress, placing the country at the forefront of Latin America in addressing the urgent challenge to reduce poverty? How was this done despite the negative impact of the internal armed conflict? Furthermore, how was this progress made in the middle of complex peace negotiations that led to the dismantling of the oldest and most powerful guerrilla group in the Western hemisphere?

The answer to these questions is undoubtedly of interest to analysts and scholars of poverty and social policy but also to government leaders, businesspeople, social leaders, and ordinary people who want to learn about the Colombian model for poverty reduction, its implementation and challenges, and the lessons it can provide for other nations, including those experiencing armed conflicts and that have to contend, like Colombia, with millions of war victims and displaced persons.

Although the twenty-first century's second decade was encouraging, we must face the fact that its third decade began tragically. The COVID-19 pandemic, declared in 2020, resulted in not only millions of deaths worldwide but also a contraction of the global economy and national economies. That contraction has translated into millions of jobs lost and vast numbers of the

---

[1] According to the methodology of the Mission for the Splicing of Employment, Poverty, and Inequality Series (MESEP in Spanish), in effect until 2018.

[2] According to the MESEP methodology.

[3] Updated percentages based on the projections of the 2018 National Population and Housing Census.

world's population falling back into poverty. Local and multilateral statistical agencies are still calculating the pandemic's social impact, but it is clear that its effects outweigh those of the Great Depression in the 1930s.

Why is it worth highlighting and recounting how progress was made in the fight against poverty in Colombia in recent years, when much of that progress was lost in a few months? There are two fundamental reasons.

First, the economic and social achievements placed the country in a better position to cope with the health crisis. Facing the new coronavirus in a country where 40 out of every 100 inhabitants are poor is not the same as facing it in a country where that figure had been reduced to 27. This is speaking in terms of monetary poverty, as the figure is less than 20 if we consider multidimensional poverty. In other words, moving backwards from an advanced position is less serious than moving backwards from a position already lagging behind. More options and better instruments are available to get back on track.

Second, now more than ever, when hundreds of millions of people and families have seen their quality of life and living conditions decrease dramatically, studying and replicating Colombia's experience has become so important. The time is right to talk about poverty and how to overcome it with committed leadership, targeted policies, and appropriate instruments.

The fight against poverty is not just a technical issue but also one of leadership. In the case of Colombia, as president, I personally took on directing and supervising social policy, and this undoubtedly made a difference. The State's social sector was run by an administrative department whose director reported directly to the president. With the support of international advisors, novel mechanisms were established to monitor progress, standstills, and setbacks in the fight against poverty, such as the Cross-Cutting Poverty Roundtable and a dashboard that evaluated each ministry and public entity's contribution to the joint goal of reducing poverty.

The official adoption of the Multidimensional Poverty Index made it possible for the Colombian government to understand and integrate different dimensions of poverty into its decisions, respond with innovative programs to warnings indicating where timely State intervention was needed, and optimize public entities' investments and social actions by directing the budget and programs to alleviate the most pressing needs of the most vulnerable population segments.

Programs for comprehensive early childhood care, free housing for the poorest people, and the expansion of health-care coverage are examples of how the State responded efficiently to the warnings that were identified by the C-MPI.

There is an undeniable relationship between poverty and violence, two scourges that, as a government leader, I became obsessed with overcoming. There can be no real development without peace, and true and lasting peace is not viable without social development. Today, Colombia is a global model of care for, and reparation of, war victims; land restitution for people who have been dispossessed; and the reintegration of former combatants into society. Its lessons, painfully learned, can be useful in many of the world's regions.

A similar situation occurred with the Sustainable Development Goals and the increasingly pressing problem of climate change, issues in which Colombia has played a leading role and which continue to be the backbone of the global agenda. The C-MPI is being used in a pioneering way to assess progress on these commitments.

In this book, I intend to share Colombia's experience, which demonstrates that, with political will, good and effective coordination, and reliable indicators, progress can be made toward a future with greater social equality. If this book can contribute even a small amount to the discussion on rebuilding a better post-pandemic world, then I will have accomplished my goal.

Juan Manuel Santos

Contents

An Important Clarification on Changes in the Measurement of Monetary and Multidimensional Poverty in Colombia

Changes in the Measurement of Monetary Poverty

At the beginning of 2020, when I started writing this book, monetary or income poverty was measured in Colombia according to a methodology that had been established by the Mission for the Splicing of Employment, Poverty, and Inequality Series (MESEP in Spanish). The MESEP was a mission of experts convened by the Colombian government at the beginning of 2009, and its work will be discussed in the first chapters of the book. Throughout my term in office, between 2010 and 2018, the National Administrative Department of Statistics (DANE in Spanish) used this methodology.

Following this methodology, we were able to observe how national monetary poverty in Colombia fell from 40.3% in 2009 to 27.0% in 2018, while extreme monetary poverty fell from 14.4% in 2009 to 7.2% in 2018. These statistics reflected the success of the economic and social policies implemented to combat poverty.

After my administration concluded, the DANE reported a change in the methodology to measure monetary poverty on September 30, 2020. This change was based on the 2016–2017 National Household Budget Survey (ENPH in Spanish), a survey conducted in the country every ten years that reflects the income and expenditure of Colombian families.

The new survey's results were made available in mid-2018 and reflected updated data on the country's household consumption baskets and a more accurate measurement of household income and expenditures, which also led to updating the methodology for calculating the extreme monetary poverty and monetary poverty lines. Among several of the factors that changed, one example is that the consumption of foods prepared outside the household was included within the basic basket.

The updating of the methodology to measure monetary poverty was headed by a Committee of Experts on Poverty made up of nine academic experts; three international institutions: the Economic Commission for Latin America and the Caribbean (ECLAC), the World Bank, and the United Nations Development Programme (UNDP); and three national entities: the DANE, the National Planning Department, and the Department for Social Prosperity.

With the new data obtained from the 2016–2017 ENPH, the poverty lines—meaning the income considered necessary to reach a minimum level of well-being—were set at a higher value, and there was a corresponding increase in the rates of monetary poverty and extreme monetary poverty. According to the Committee, "the incorporated methodological changes offer greater accuracy by capturing broader territorial heterogeneity and recognizing the consumption habits of each geographical domain, as well as changes in household consumption patterns" (Comité de Expertos en Pobreza, 2020).

Notably, this updated methodology has not been exclusive to Colombia. Other countries in Latin America, such as Chile (2015), Paraguay (2017), and Honduras (2019), have done the same.

In this context, while national monetary poverty in 2018 was estimated at 27.0% using the MESEP methodology, it increased to 34.7% with the Committee of Experts on Poverty's updated methodology. The extreme poverty rate was also recalculated from 7.2% to 8.2% for this same year.

In a communiqué on October 13, 2020, the Committee of Experts on Poverty recommended that the DANE:

1. Publish monetary poverty and extreme poverty results for the 2012–2019 period, considering the updated poverty lines based on the 2016–2017 ENPH.
2. Maintain the series corresponding to the baskets of the Mission for the Splicing of Employment, Poverty, and Inequality Series (MESEP) methodology during a period of two years, with the aim of enabling the comparability of the change in values in the series due to the updated methodology.

(Comité de Expertos en Pobreza, 2020)

This two-year period for maintaining the series according to the MESEP methodology corresponds to 2019 and 2020.

Taking these recommendations into account, the DANE has published a comparison between the data obtained with the MESEP methodology and the data obtained with the updated methodology between 2012 and 2021, as follows:

Table 1 Comparison between monetary poverty and extreme poverty rates obtained with MESEP methodology and those obtained with the methodology updated by the Committee of Experts on Poverty, 2012–2021

Year	Monetary poverty (MESEP) (%)	Monetary poverty (updated methodology) (%)	Extreme monetary poverty (MESEP) (%)	Extreme monetary poverty (updated methodology) (%)
2012	32.7	40.8	10.4	11.7
2013	30.6	38.3	9.1	10.0
2014	28.5	36.3	8.1	9.4
2015	27.8	36.1	7.9	9.1
2016	28.0	36.2	8.5	9.9
2017	26.9	35.2	7.4	8.4
2018	27.0	34.7	7.2	8.2
2019	28.2	35.7	8.7	9.6
2020	35.4	42.5	13.6	15.1
2021	N/a	39.3	N/a	12.2

Source: DANE (2022a).

As can be seen, the series was updated beginning in 2012, which means that there is no comparable data before that year. For the same reason, and taking into account that this book's purpose is to offer an explanation and some lessons about the poverty reduction process between 2009 and 2018, for practical purposes, the data calculated with the MESEP methodology will be used in several cases, with corresponding annotations indicating this is being done. Similarly, it will be noted when data based on the updated methodology from the Committee of Experts on Poverty is used.

The following are the monetary poverty and extreme monetary poverty rates reported by the DANE from 2002 until 2011, calculated with the MESEP methodology, which have no equivalents in the new updated methodology:

Table 2 Monetary poverty and extreme poverty
rates reported by the DANE, 2002–2011

Year	Monetary poverty (MESEP) (%)	Extreme monetary poverty (MESEP) (%)
2002	49.7	17.7
2003	48.0	15.7
2004	47.4	14.8
2005	45.0	13.8
2006	N/a	N/a
2007	N/a	N/a
2008	42.0	16.4
2009	40.3	14.4
2010	37.2	12.3
2011	34.1	10.6

Source: DANE (2019).

Changes in the Measurement of Multidimensional Poverty

This book is mainly about the incorporation of the Colombian Multidimensional Poverty Index (C-MPI) and its contribution to reducing poverty. Considering that a new population census was conducted in Colombia in 2018 (the previous one had been in 2005), the official figures on multidimensional poverty between 2010 and 2018 were recalculated according to the projections of the 2018 National Population and Housing Census. Therefore, they are not comparable with the figures calculated based on the population projections of the 2005 General Census. From 2019 onwards, the index has been calculated exclusively using the projections of the 2018 census. It should be noted that, due to methodological problems in the National Quality of Life Survey, the C-MPI was not calculated for 2017, and only the figures for municipal seats are available.

As was done with the change in the monetary poverty methodology, the DANE updated the multidimensional poverty series from previous years for purposes of comparability. The C-MPI was recalculated from 2010 until 2018 based on the 2018 census projections so that it could be compared with the figures that were based on the 2005 census projections. Thus, the DANE reports the following data from the Colombian Multidimensional Poverty Index between 2010 and 2021:

Table 3 Comparison of Colombian Multidimensional Poverty Index data using 2005 census projections and 2018 census projections, 2010–2021

Year	MPI (calculated using 2005 census projections) (%)	MPI (calculated using 2018 census projections) (%)
2010	30.4	29.7
2011	29.4	28.8
2012	27.0	26.5
2013	24.8	24.3
2014	21.9	21.6
2015	20.2	19.8
2016	17.8	17.6
2017	N/a	N/a
2018	19.6	19.1
2019	N/a	17.5
2020	N/a	18.1
2021	N/a	16.0

Source: DANE (2022b).

The Year 2020: A Pandemic Anomaly

As for the data on monetary poverty and multidimensional poverty in 2020, an exceptional situation must be taken into account: the COVID-19 pandemic. This pandemic was declared in 2020 and had its greatest economic and social impact in that year. Due to this pandemic and the restrictions on conducting fieldwork for the surveys, the DANE had to adapt part of its information collection methods. This was done mainly by analyzing administrative records.

It is clear to everyone that poverty increased sharply not only in Colombia but also in all countries worldwide as a result of this health emergency, which, as I write these words in mid-2022, has not been entirely resolved. The impacts of COVID-19 on global poverty cannot be underestimated. Some say that, given the major social and economic setbacks, the world could be facing a lost decade for development (Inter-Agency Task Force, 2021; UNICEF, 2021). However, this crisis, as every crisis, can be an opportunity to redouble efforts and renew national and international leadership in the fight against poverty. Maybe this time we will do it better.

References

Comité de Expertos En Pobreza. (2020). "Declaración del Comité de Expertos en Pobreza, octubre 13 de 2020. Publicación de pobreza monetaria extrema y pobreza monetaria." October 13. https://www.dane.gov.co/files/investigaciones/condiciones_vida/pobreza/2019/Comunicado-expertos-pobreza-monetaria_2019.pdf.

DANE (National Administrative Department of Statistics). (2019). "Comunicado de prensa. Pobreza monetaria. Año 2018." May 3. https://www.dane.gov.co/files/investigaciones/condiciones_vida/pobreza/2018/cp_pobreza_monetaria_18.pdf.

DANE. (2022a). "Comunicado de prensa. Pobreza monetaria. Año 2021." April 26. https://www.dane.gov.co/files/investigaciones/condiciones_vida/pobreza/2021/Comunicado-pobreza-monetaria_2021.pdf.

DANE. (2022b). "Pobreza y desigualdad. Pobreza multidimensional." April 28. https://www.dane.gov.co/index.php/estadisticas-por-tema/pobreza-y-condiciones-de-vida/pobreza-multidimensional.

Inter-Agency Task Force on Financing for Development. (2021). "Financing for sustainable development report 2021." United Nations. https://developmentfinance.un.org/fsdr2021.

UNICEF (United Nations International Children's Fund). (2021). "Preventing a lost decade: Urgent action to reverse the devastating impact of COVID-19 on children and young people." UNICEF. https://www.unicef.org/reports/unicef-75-preventing-a-lost-decade.

List of Tables

Introduction

A Commitment to Poverty Reduction

An Unforgettable Lesson

The distinguished professor, only 41 years old, entered the classroom where we were eagerly awaiting his first lecture. It was 1975, and I was just another student, only 23 years old myself, sitting in a classroom at the London School of Economics (LSE). I'd graduated from the University of Kansas with a business and economics degree and was now living in London, where I worked as a representative of Colombia to the International Coffee Organization. Taking advantage of my stay in the English capital, I enrolled in a master's degree program in economic development at this prestigious university, fulfilling a dream that I'd had for years.

It was not just any professor who taught us that day. His name was Amartya Sen, the famous Indian economist who had taught in Kolkata, Cambridge and New Delhi and who was now lecturing at LSE. Just two years earlier, he had published one of his most impactful books, *On Economic Inequality*, at an Oxford press. In the book, he posited the need to measure poverty in a way beyond statistical or quantitative estimates, which would contribute to explaining and combating it in its various dimensions.

Professor Sen—I remember very well—began his lecture by bringing up a case study to his students. It was about a farmer who had a herd of cows and produced milk for sale, which he stored in several canteens. One day, some peasants from the region stole one of his canteens, and they were consequently arrested and put on trial. Sen's first question to his students was, "Do you believe these people should be convicted for what they did?" The answer was unanimous. We all raised our hands, delivering our verdict: "Guilty."

Professor Sen continued. He told us to keep thinking about the same case— the same farmer, the same milk canteens, the same theft—but said he was going to give us additional information. The farmer in the example was a rich, powerful man with a monopoly on milk in the area, and he was in the habit of manipulating product supply to keep prices high. Often, when he had

The Battle Against Poverty. Juan Manuel Santos, Oxford University Press.
© Juan Manuel Santos (2023). DOI: 10.1093/oso/9780192885234.003.0001

surplus product, he would store the excess milk in the canteens and, when it spoiled after a certain time, would dump it into the river. Some of his neighbors became aware of this practice, and members of a very poor family, whose young children were hungry and malnourished, decided to steal one of the canteens to use the milk before the miserly farmer threw it out.

"After receiving this information," Sen asked, "how many of you would convict the thieves for their actions?" Only one or two students raised their hands. The rest of us remained silent, taking in the profound lesson he had just taught us.

This was more than just a story about poverty. It was an example of how economics and ethics intersect in real life and the dilemmas this poses. Indeed, Professor Sen has been recognized for including ethical issues in economic affairs as one of his greatest contributions to the economic and social sciences.

I bring up this memory because that first encounter with this great philosopher and economist marked the beginning of a relationship that, years later, would yield concrete results in combating poverty in my country, Colombia, which is the topic I will address in this book.

In 1988, I was fortunate to take classes once again with Professor Sen, this time at Harvard University, where I was a Nieman fellow, part of a special program for journalists. By then, he had already proposed his theory of human development, which places people at the center of the concept of development. This theory influenced the creation of the Human Development Index, calculated by the United Nations Development Programme (UNDP) since 1990. With ample merits, Sen was awarded the 1998 Nobel Prize in Economics for this and other outstanding contributions to welfare economics. More recently, in his role as a senior advisor at the Oxford Poverty and Human Development Initiative (OPHI), he has been the inspiration and main advocate for the Multidimensional Poverty Index (MPI), which uses a methodology established by economists Sabina Alkire, OPHI's current director, and James Foster.

More than 35 years after that memorable class in 1975 in an LSE classroom, I was able to close the cycle that had begun with Professor Sen's lesson. As the president of Colombia, I adopted and implemented the MPI in my country. I'm proud to say that we—along with Mexico and Bhutan—were pioneers in this decision.

Today, when I remember that long-ago class, I marvel at the coincidences that brought our lives together. I think about that curious young man, my 23-year-old self. I imagine how astonished he would have been if I'd told him then that, decades later, he would share two characteristics with that acclaimed professor who stimulated our minds with his astute questions: both of us would receive the Nobel Prize—in my case, the Peace Prize— and both, as co-founders, would promote the Multidimensional Poverty Peer Network that he inspired.

First Contacts with Poverty

I was born in Bogotá into a family with a long tradition in Colombia's political and economic history. My great-great-grandaunt Antonia Santos was a heroine in the struggle for independence from Spain. As a result of her revolutionary activity, she was shot to death in July 1819 by the Spanish. My granduncle Eduardo Santos was the owner of the country's most influential newspaper, *El Tiempo*, and was the president of Colombia between 1938 and 1942. My grandfather Enrique Santos Montejo, known by his pen name, Calibán, was a very well-regarded journalist and the nation's most popular columnist, and my father, Enrique Santos Castillo, was the managing editor of *El Tiempo* for nearly 60 years until his death in 2001.

I am part of a privileged social class, one consisting of a few families who have held power and wealth in our country for decades, if not centuries. Nevertheless, I grew up in an atmosphere of relative frugality because of my mother, Clemencia Calderón, who taught me the value of money and who, more than anyone else, instilled a sense of solidarity, austerity, and compassion in me.

My mother belonged to an affluent family, particularly on the side of my grandmother Teresa Nieto. However, the Nieto family members were gamblers at heart (I inherited this somewhat, but in the good, analytical-poker-player sense), and they lost their wealth gambling. My grandmother was left in a precarious economic situation and was forced to send my mother, still a child, to live with the Cano family, who, paradoxically, owned the second most influential newspaper in the country, *El Espectador*. She simply didn't have the resources to support her daughter.

Perhaps that childhood experience is what forged my mother's character and gave her that sense for saving and frugality that she taught all of us as her children. We lacked for nothing at home, but we also never flaunted anything. Discipline, work, frugality, and study were the most respected values, considered to be the only ones that could ensure success in life. My grandmother Teresa, despite her economic turmoil, never stopped thinking about others and devoted a significant amount of time to volunteering, including to help improve the conditions of prostitutes. As for my mother, she contributed to the fight against tuberculosis as part of the Colombia Anti-Tuberculosis League, which she chaired for a time. For years, she was also a board member at the Hospital Lorencita Villegas de Santos, which provided health care for children from the lowest-income families.

It is impossible to avoid being exposed to poverty in a country like Colombia, where a large proportion of the population lives without the minimum conditions of dignity that all human beings deserve. In the 1960s, when I was in grade school, it was common to see gangs of children on the street, parentless kids who slept on the sidewalks and inhaled Boxer, a brand of rubber-based glue that, after being inhaled, produced a mixture of euphoria and sleepiness that helped them to ward off hunger. Those children, who would steal watches and jewelry from unsuspecting passers-by, were known in Spanish as *gamines* (from the French word *gamin*) and became a kind of Bogotá identity marker at the time.

In my case, as an avid reader from a very young age, one book in particular made me reflect on poverty and solidarity with people who had the least: *Heart*, by the Italian author Edmondo de Amicis. In this book, Enrico, a boy attending a municipal school in Turin, tells the story of his classmates. They include some children from well-off or middle-class families but also a stonemason's son, a coal miner's son, a boy with a paralyzed arm, and a boy with a hunchback. Thanks to its simple and compassionate prose, many young readers like myself learned to value others beyond their social status or their disabilities.

I had my first direct contact with poverty on my grandfather Calibán's farm in Cajicá, a small town on the outskirts of Bogotá. As a child, I loved going there, where I could play in the fields and run around freely. My best friend was the son of the farm's keeper, and he was the same age as me. We often ended up playing in his parents' house, a humble adobe construction at the edge of the estate. There, I was astonished by how their living conditions were so different than mine in the city. The spaces were much smaller, the kitchen was attached to the only bedroom, and there was a dirt floor and a wood stove. They didn't have water or electricity. Back then, I didn't think much about it, being more entertained with our games, but that image has stuck with me.

When I finished my fourth year of secondary school at Colegio San Carlos, I made a decision that would put me in more direct contact with the harsh reality of life: I left school in Bogotá to finish my last two years at the Cartagena Naval Academy as a cadet. There, I adapted to military discipline and learned not only the art of navigation, which includes principles that have served me my entire life, but also about the social situation in other regions of the country. On days off, I walked with my fellow cadets through the streets and markets of Cartagena, a beautiful city on the Caribbean coast but one that has tremendous extreme poverty rates. I especially remember Chambacú, a neighborhood on the outskirts of the famous historic city center that hero-ically resisted attacks by British ships, including those of Sir Francis Drake in the sixteenth century and those of Admiral Edward Vernon in the eigh-teenth century, who aimed to take control of that important commercial port. Afro-Colombian people were the main residents of this neighborhood, where poverty was so rampant that it was known as the "largest slum in Colombia." Living conditions were subhuman, and as a result, residents were moved to other areas of the city in the early 1970s.

There was poverty in Chambacú, but also life, joy, and happiness amidst the misery. There, beautiful Black women from the Caribbean taught me to dance, an activity that doesn't come very naturally to those of us born in the country's mountainous interior. I also tasted the best fish *sancocho* (a tradi-tional Colombian soup) of my life. Another lesson to take in: human warmth rises above economic deprivation.

After the Naval Academy, I went to the University of Kansas, where I stud-ied business and economics. I arrived in Kansas in 1969, when the words spoken by Robert F. Kennedy on March 18, 1968, at the Allen Fieldhouse, the university's events venue, as he began his race for the Democratic Party nomination, were still echoing in the hearts of students and professors there. Kennedy gave a memorable speech about student protests, the senselessness of the Vietnam War, and poverty. He spoke, without euphemisms, about the starving children in Mississippi and the precarious conditions of Native American and Black people in his country. It was also a masterful speech about social justice. I read it many times while studying in Kansas, and his words sunk into my spirit, including his remarks underscoring that the wealth of a people is not measured by their goods and services but by their quality of life and values:

even if we act to erase material poverty, there is another greater task; it is to confront the poverty of satisfaction—purpose and dignity—that afflicts us all. Too much and for too long, we seemed to have surrendered personal excellence and community values in the mere accumulation of material things. Our Gross National Product, now, is over $800 billion dollars a year, but that Gross National Product—if we judge the United States of America by that—that Gross National Product counts air pollution and cigarette advertising, and ambulances to clear our highways of carnage [...] Yet the gross national product does not allow for the health of our children, the quality of their education or the joy of their play. It does not include the beauty of our poetry or the strength of our marriages, the intelligence of our public debate or the integrity of our public officials. It measures neither our wit nor our courage, neither our wisdom nor our learning, neither our compassion nor our devotion to our country. It measures everything in short, except that which makes life worthwhile. And it can tell us everything about America except why we are proud that we are Americans. If this is true here at home, so it is true elsewhere in world.

(Kennedy, 1968)

In his very personal style, Bobby Kennedy, a true visionary, was proposing a new way of gauging the progress of peoples, something that would leave a mark on my thinking. Tragically, for the United States and for the world, this great leader was assassinated two-and-a-half months after delivering this speech.

Experiences as a Journalist and Public Servant

In July 2005, I had the opportunity to fulfill a postponed dream: to make the pilgrimage along at least a part of the famous Camino de Santiago. This route, known in English as the Way of St James, includes rural paths from various countries that lead to the imposing cathedral of Santiago de Compostela, capital of the community of Galicia in Spain, where they say the remains of St James the Apostle lie. I traveled the Portuguese route, walking seven hours a day, which gave me time to reflect and observe. But I did more than that: during my pilgrimage, I also took advantage of the opportunity to write and send in a weekly column that I published in *El Tiempo*.

In my column, I wrote about how I saw many Portuguese and Spanish farmers with their herds of cattle as I was walking along this historic route. I reflected on the fact that a single one of their cows, hardy and well fed, received more in subsidies than what a Colombian day laborer and their family earn, all because of the European Union's agricultural and livestock policy. Around that time, the eight leaders of the planet's most powerful countries (the G8) had met in Scotland and discussed how to alleviate poverty in Africa as well as the need to take action to stop climate change. That's right: climate change was already a topic of summit meetings back then, though unfortunately real actions were never seen.

I thought, as I gazed at those fortunate cows, that rich countries' gesture of forgiving the poorest countries' debt and committing a higher budget to foreign aid was important, but it was far from being enough. Just like people, nations make more, and better, progress by producing resources, not receiving them. That only helps to strengthen dependence. Therefore, I concluded in my column, support to achieve inclusive growth and create good jobs is what is required to combat poverty, more so than monetary aid. According to the Chinese proverb, you should teach people how to fish instead of giving them a fish.

With articles like this, poverty, and the need to create mechanisms to combat it, became one of my favorite topics as a journalist as well as my profession and a vocation that runs through my veins. When I returned to Colombia in the early 1980s, after living for nearly a decade in London and after earning a master's degree in public administration from the John F. Kennedy School of Government at Harvard University, I joined my family's newspaper. There, I worked as deputy director while also keeping up a weekly column and writing editorials.

Journalism was the ideal profession to stay up to date on the problems in Colombia and the world, with poverty being one of the most historically pressing. It is impossible to practice journalism—good journalism—without becoming aware of issues such as inequality and violence, which were the order of the day in my country.

Nevertheless, a different path was awaiting me in public service. President César Gaviria invited me to join his administration as the country's first minister of foreign trade, and so I left *El Tiempo*, where I would return as a columnist one day. From then on, I immersed myself in the hard and challenging work of politics and government.

I was Colombia's first minister of foreign trade, from 1991 to 1994, in charge of opening the economy to a more globalized world; after that, I was minister of finance from 2000 to 2002 under the Andrés Pastrana administration, when I had to navigate and mitigate the effects of the worst economic crisis in the past century; and finally, I was minister of defense from 2006 to 2009 under the Álvaro Uribe administration. Based on my active participation in the respective cabinets, and obviously also my work in each of the sectors that I was responsible for, I gained a deep knowledge of the country, its regions, and its needs.

As minister of finance, for example, I was in charge of the distribution and execution of the national budget, always scarce in the face of urgent social needs. I understood precisely how each administration's priorities were reflected in their budget allocations to the respective sectors. I have always said that, in government, love is shown in the budget. This was a lesson that

I put into practice later on as president, when I gave the education sector the largest budget, greater than that of the defense and security sector, which had traditionally received the most funding. This had never happened before in Colombia.

During my time as minister of defense, I faced an enormous challenge: to lead the greatest military and police offensive deployed up until then against the guerrilla forces and narco-terrorist cartels. We had great success, and there is consensus that, in those years, the balance of military power in the long war waged between the guerrillas and the State shifted in favor of the State. As a result, the Revolutionary Armed Forces of Colombia (FARC) understood that they would never achieve their objectives through armed warfare and accepted negotiating a peace agreement that led to their demobilization.

But war is not an end in itself; to me, it was a means to achieve a greater good: peace. I never felt joy at the death of guerrilla fighters and criminals who fell in the different operations I led as minister. I knew we were doing the right thing, but I also knew, deep inside, that each life lost was the life of a Colombian, lives of mostly poor young men who, due to the lack of opportunities, or sometimes because they were forced, had gone down the wrong path of violence. In Colombia, and in the world, those who fight, those who risk everything, those who die are always the poorest people, both in regular armies and in illegal armed groups.

Therefore, as minister, I instructed the military to radically change its doctrine and mode of operation in combat. It was accustomed to a terrible system of "body counting" that became famous in the Vietnam War, which measures success by the number of dead bodies from enemy forces. I told the military that from then on, to measure operations' success, a demobilized guerrilla would have a greater value than a captured guerrilla and a captured guerrilla would have a greater value than a dead guerrilla. I went even further by issuing the Comprehensive Policy on Human Rights and International Humanitarian Law, which framed State warfare within the parameters of humanity and compassion.

During my years as minister of defense, I had to attend many funerals and hug and comfort many mothers and widows mourning their loved ones. These were tragic, devastating moments, and each time, I made a firm resolution that I sought to make a reality later on: this senseless war between children of the same nation must be stopped. It was a war being fought by the poorest Colombians, which, in turn, produced more poverty due to the dynamics of terror and intimidation in the country's towns and countryside.

"We Will Not Fail the Poor in Colombia"

What greater honor and privilege than to be elected to lead the future of a country? My life experiences led me, as a logical next step in my personal journey and public career, to accept a nomination for president for the 2010–2014 term in Colombia. My fellow citizens knew me for my work as a journalist and for my performance at the three ministries I had led, especially the Ministry of Defense, where my popularity had grown to unprecedented levels. It is always more popular and easier to make war than to make peace, and I would realize this firsthand in the following years.

On June 20, 2010, I was elected president of Colombia, with the support of over 9 million citizens, the highest number of votes received in a presidential election up until then. My government platform, which I summarized in 110 initiatives, began with the following paragraph:

> Our efforts will be directed toward the people, and especially to the Colombians most in need. Our main goal is for Colombians and their families on August 7, 2014, to be able to say, "We are better off than we were four years ago!"
>
> (Santos, 2010a, p. 5)

It was very clear to me that poverty reduction had to be my administration's first task, and therefore over half of my campaign proposals were social initiatives. In fact, the title of the first chapter in my government platform stated it clearly: "Our Priority: The Fight against Poverty."

In this document, I proposed, for example, maintaining and improving conditional assistance programs to encourage parents to send their children to school, as well as strengthening the network of social workers—I called them my "social army"—who supported the most vulnerable families on their path out of poverty. I also promised to improve access to the health system and a more equitable distribution of resources in the regions.

My predecessor's administration had been characterized by prioritizing security, and it was known as the "democratic security" administration. In my case, without disregarding this aspect, I wanted to emphasize the need for democratizing wealth, and therefore I coined the term "democratic prosperity." My campaign priorities revolved around three goals: more jobs, more security, and less poverty. These became my focus.

On the afternoon of August 7, 2010, before a crowded Plaza de Bolívar in Bogotá, including many foreign heads of state, I took office as president of Colombia. On that same morning, I had been in the Sierra Nevada de Santa Marta, a mountain range with great diversity in the north of the country, for a symbolic inauguration ceremony officiated by the *mamos*—the elders, spiritual leaders—of the Indigenous peoples who live in that marvelous region. They gave me a traditional wooden baton and entrusted me with two tasks: to make peace among Colombians and to make peace with Mother Earth, who, in their words, was angry and sick due to mistreatment by humans.

At the official inauguration, after being bestowed with the presidential sash, I delivered my inaugural address, in which I set the course for my administration. Standing before the special guests and, more importantly, before the millions of Colombians who were following the ceremony on the radio and television, I firmly expressed my commitment to the fight against poverty:

> The time has come for the natural assets that were granted to us so abundantly, assets that we Colombians have multiplied with ingenuity and good sense, to no longer be the privilege of a few but rather within the reach of many.
>
> That is the core meaning of democratic prosperity. A dignified house, a stable job with a fair salary and benefits, access to education and health care. Basic well-being, with economic peace of mind, for every Colombian family.
>
> Only then, when no Colombian wakes up in the morning uncertain about their daily sustenance, only then will the existence of a society with collective strength, capable of dreaming a common future, be possible.
>
> If we overcome the challenge of poverty, Colombia's intellectual and economic potential will take off as an unstoppable force.
>
> That's why I reiterate today, before the watchful statue of the Liberator, that we will not let the poor down. We will not fail the poor in Colombia!
>
> (Santos, 2010b)

References

Kennedy, R. F. (1968). "Remarks at the University of Kansas, March 18, 1968" [speech transcript]. John F. Kennedy Presidential Library and Museum. https://www.jfklibrary.org/learn/about-jfk/the-kennedy-family/robert-f-kennedy/robert-f-kennedy-speeches/remarks-at-the-university-of-kansas-march-18-1968.

Santos, J. M. (2010a). "Buen Gobierno para la Prosperidad Democrática. 110 iniciativas para lograrla." https://redescolombia.files.wordpress.com/2010/08/plan-de-gobierno-juan-manuel-santos-09-34-50.pdf.

Santos, J. M. (2010b). "Discurso completo de posesión de Juan Manuel Santos" [speech transcript]. *Semana*, 7 August. https://www.semana.com/politica/articulo/discurso-completo-posesion-juan-manuel-santos/120293-3.

Sen, A. (1973). *On economic inequality*. Clarendon Press.

1

A New Measurement of Poverty

Multidimensional Poverty Index: A New Approach

In the history of both natural and social sciences, there are times when chance and willingness come together, creating positive effects called to transform society and the world. One of these times was in December 2006, at the University of Oxford, when Sabina Alkire and James Foster brought together their experiences and knowledge to work on an exceptional proposal. During a week of intense and productive discussions, these innovative and inquisitive economists constructed a comprehensive methodology for measuring multidimensional poverty that led to the creation of the Multidimensional Poverty Index (MPI).

This joint effort resulted in a working paper titled "Counting and Multidimensional Poverty Measurement" (Alkire and Foster, 2007), published by the recently established Oxford Poverty and Human Development Initiative (OPHI) in December 2007. The methodology proposed in this paper—published as an academic article in 2011 (Alkire and Foster, 2011)—became known as the Alkire–Foster method and is the basis for the global MPI adopted by the United Nations Development Programme (UNDP) and various national MPIs, including Colombia's pioneering C-MPI.

Who are these scholars who proposed this transformative step not only to improve poverty measurement but also, more importantly, to reduce poverty more effectively?

In 1984, as a student at Cornell, James Foster—holding a degree in economics and mathematics from New College, Florida, as well as a PhD in economics from Cornell University—coauthored and published an article on an income poverty measure that became one of the most cited and influential articles on the subject (Foster et al., 1984).[1] Since then, his academic career has been focused on this topic. He held a position as a professor of economics at Vanderbilt University and is currently a professor of international affairs and economics at the George Washington University.

---

[1] This article was subsequently reprinted in *Measurement of Inequality and Poverty* (edited by S. Subramanian), Oxford University Press, 1998; and *Development Economics: Critical Concepts in Development Studies* (edited by C. Barrett), Routledge, 2007.

The Battle Against Poverty. Juan Manuel Santos, Oxford University Press. © Juan Manuel Santos (2023). DOI: 10.1093/oso/9780192885234.003.0002

Sabina Alkire holds a BA in sociology from the University of Illinois as well as a master's degree in Christian political ethics, another master's in economics for development, and a PhD in economics (with all three graduate degrees from the University of Oxford). She is a co-founder and the current director of OPHI.

It is important to highlight Dr Alkire's affinity with Professor Amartya Sen's ideas, to the point that she devoted her master's thesis (Alkire, 1995) and dissertation (Alkire, 1998) to demonstrating the applicability of the conceptual work of this Indian philosopher and economist—a true champion of human development—to poverty measurement and concrete actions for poverty reduction.[2] In her field work in Pakistan, for example, she applied Sen's ideas to analyze the various dimensions of living conditions, beyond monetary income alone, that determine whether a person is poor.

In mid-2006, Alkire, who, at the time, was conducting a study in India on women's empowerment, attended a lecture in Manchester where Foster spoke on the issue of chronic poverty. She was impressed by the clarity of his presentation and envisioned applying his theses to multiple dimensions. In December 2006, she invited him to Oxford, where she was organizing OPHI's establishment. It was there, at that historic university, which has made so many valuable contributions to the sciences and human welfare, that they met and brought their visions together.

Thus, the Multidimensional Poverty Index was born, as well as the Alkire–Foster method to calculate and apply it. The authors introduced their methodology for the first time at OPHI's launch in 2007. It was favorably received by the academic world, and studies were soon published in several Latin American countries, as well as in China, Bhutan, and Uganda, where economists began to apply the methodology experimentally in the field.[3]

Pioneering Experiments

OPHI's first government interaction took place with the government of Mexico, which had already advanced work on multidimensional poverty.[4] Mexico began measuring income poverty in the early 2000s, but the fact that the government, through its Ministry of Social Development (Secretaría de

---

[2] In her work, Sabina Alkire exhaustively reviewed everything Sen had written up to that time, from philosophy and social choice theory to economics and development.

[3] See, e.g. the literature on Bhutan (Santos, 2013), Sub-Saharan Africa (Batana, 2013), China (Yu, 2013), Latin America (Battiston et al., 2013), and India (Alkire and Seth, 2013). These and other relevant articles may be found in Social Indicators Research, 112(2), 2013.

[4] See "In Mexico, social policy has focused on multidimensional measurement" (MPPN, 2016).

Desarrollo Social), did so directly raised multiple suspicions that the data could be used or manipulated to serve the political interests of incumbent government leaders. Thus, in January 2004, during the term of President Vicente Fox, the Mexican Congress decided that henceforth poverty should be measured more independently and that multidimensional criteria should be used. For this purpose, as well as for the autonomous evaluation of social programs and policies, the General Law of Social Development was enacted, which created the National Council for the Evaluation of Social Development Policy (CONEVAL in Spanish), a decentralized public entity.

Following this, a rigorous multiyear process to establish a methodology began, culminating at the end of 2009. This process sought out advice and guidance from five teams of international experts, including James Foster, who later invited Sabina Alkire, in addition to researchers from the World Bank and the United Nations. The result was Mexico's Multidimensional Poverty Measure, officially adopted in December 2009 by the Mexican government, led by Felipe Calderón. This measure includes seven dimensions established by the law: (1) current income per capita, (2) average household educational deficit, (3) access to health services, (4) access to social security, (5) dignified and decent housing quality and size, (6) access to basic services in dignified and decent housing, and (7) access to nutritious and quality food. They are reported alongside two independently calculated indicators: degree of social cohesion and degree of access to paved roads (Ley General de Desarrollo Social, 2018).[5]

What Mexico accomplished in constructing its own multidimensional poverty measure was a very important step for the region and for the world.[6] Nevertheless, despite having received advice from Foster and Alkire, as well as from OPHI, this MPI is not fully based on the Alkire–Foster methodology. Instead, the official measure focuses on the headcount ratio obtained by dividing the number of people identified as poor by the total number of people in society.

Simultaneously, a similar process, albeit with different objectives, was taking place in a small Asian country in the foothills of the Himalayas, situated between China and India. I am referring to the Kingdom of Bhutan, a nation with a culture and legal system based on Buddhist principles. This focus on spirituality entails having criteria for evaluating a society's progress that

---

[5] The degree of social cohesion and the degree of access to paved roads, which were added by law in 2018, are independently calculated indicators, not integrated into the multidimensional poverty measure.
[6] Additional information on Mexico's multidimensional poverty measure may be found in CONEVAL (2018, 2019).

differ from those of other societies that emphasize wealth and economic well-being. In an exceptional way, Bhutan decided to measure government goals not by economic growth but by happiness—a concept as idealistic as it is revolutionary.

Although the term "Gross National Happiness" had been in use in Bhutan since the 1970s, it was only in 2008, during the reign of Jigme Singye Wangchuck, the fourth king of Bhutan, that a representative national study was carried out, leading to the construction of a Gross National Happiness Index with a special characteristic: its multidimensional nature. The index was designed using a special adaptation of the Alkire–Foster methodology in collaboration with OPHI. It originally established 72 indicators, grouped in 9 domains such as psychological well-being, time use, good governance, community vitality, and ecological diversity and resilience. An updated index was released with district-level disaggregation using data from 2010, and once again in 2015. Both updated indices established 33 indicators. Bhutan, the kingdom that measures happiness, has thus become a model to be studied around the world—a world so accustomed to measuring well-being based solely on economic or material criteria (Ura et al., 2012, 2015). How revolutionary it would be for more countries to include criteria on people's spiritual or mental well-being in their statistics and programs!

In 2010, Bhutan published its first MPI, also based on the Alkire–Foster method, and it was presented as part of a report from a roundtable of international bodies in the country.[7] Two years later, in 2012, the Bhutanese National Statistics Bureau began officially calculating this MPI. Tshering Tobgay, the prime minister of Bhutan between 2013 and 2018, became a determined driver of this index. I met him by chance in early 2019 in the Antilles, on Necker Island, the property of entrepreneur and innovator Richard Branson. Without us being aware of it, a common bond brought us together: we had both been pioneers in making an MPI official in our countries. We now have plans to work together to promote it worldwide.

Indeed, in 2011, more than 16,000 kilometers away from Bhutan, in the northern corner of South America, Colombia was the first country to officially adopt an MPI calculated with the Alkire–Foster method and with advice from OPHI. As president, I had the privilege of making and implementing this decision, and I am proud of what has been achieved so far.

This was how, on the one hand, Mexico (employing its own calculation methods) and, on the other hand, Bhutan and Colombia (using OPHI's

---

[7] For more information on Bhutan's MPI, see National Statistics Bureau, Royal Government of Bhutan (2013) and OPHI (2017).

formula) became the first three countries to design and officially adopt multidimensional poverty indices. We were pioneers in a long list of countries—more than 60—that today make up the growing Multidimensional Poverty Peer Network (MPPN).[8]

From Unsatisfied Basic Needs to the MPI

In 1979, Argentinian economist Óscar Altimir—at the time, director of the Economic Commission for Latin America and the Caribbean's (ECLAC's) Division for Statistics and Quantitative Analysis—produced "The Extent of Poverty in Latin America," a paper that shook the foundations of poverty measurement in the region. In it, he introduced a method for measuring poverty based on unsatisfied basic needs (UBN), which could complement the traditional poverty measure based solely on monetary income.

In Altimir's words:

> In the final instance, the idea of poverty is based on value judgments as to what the minimum adequate levels of welfare and the absolutely essential basic needs are and what degree of deprivation is intolerable. Such judgments consequently imply a reference to some norm of the basic needs and their satisfaction which makes it possible to distinguish between those who are poor and those who are not.
>
> (Altimir, 1982, p. 10)

Further on, he states:

> When the goal is to satisfy basic needs [. . .] the extent to which the whole style of development must be recast if poverty is to be eliminated is thrown into greater relief. Furthermore, the actions involved affect not only the incomes of the poor, but also—and very particularly—their access to key social services. Generally speaking, special importance is given to channeling specific resources toward specific groups, with more emphasis on the nature of what is provided than on income.
>
> (Altimir, 1982, p. 21)

The influence of Amartya Sen's ideas on Altimir is clear. At the time, Sen had already published important papers on poverty measurement, of which

---

[8] The MPPN's participating countries are at different stages of developing multidimensional poverty indices. Some countries have had an MPI for years, while others are at an early stage of MPI design and adoption.

Altimir cites two: "Poverty: An Ordinal Approach to Measurement" (Sen, 1976) and "Three Notes on the Concept of Poverty" (Sen, 1978), the latter published by the International Labor Organization.

Backed by ECLAC, an organization with approaches that resonated strongly throughout the Latin America region, Altimir's ideas were widely welcomed. Thus, in the 1980s and 1990s, Latin America became, in a way, a pioneering region on the issue of multidimensional poverty with respect to a "basic needs approach."

The national statistical offices of most countries in the region began to measure and integrate various indicators on UBNs. Therefore, Mexico and Colombia did not start from scratch when they officially adopted multidimensional poverty measures or indices in 2010 and 2011. In the decades before that, they had gained important experience and collected a large amount of comparable data to feed into the new measurement. Not surprisingly, these two countries were soon followed by others in the region: Chile, El Salvador, and Costa Rica, which introduced official MPIs in 2015; and Ecuador and Honduras, which did so in 2016.

In Colombia, in particular, following ECLAC's postulates and later with support from the UNDP, we had developed an important tradition of multidimensional indicators of social well-being, especially since the mid-1990s.

Like most countries in Latin America, Colombia had an Unsatisfied Basic Needs Index based on census information, which served to identify the critical unmet needs of the country's population. Although this method is more about characterizing than measuring poverty, it complements other indicators to measure poverty.[9] Together with Mexico and Chile, Colombia led the development of UBN-based poverty maps.[10]

In addition, Colombia had a Living Conditions Index (LCI), calculated by the National Administrative Department of Statistics (DANE in Spanish) based on the National Quality of Life Survey, which quantifies and characterizes poor and non-poor Colombians' quality of life with respect to issues such as housing, utility services, education, employment, expenses, and income.[11] This index is also not a poverty measure, strictly speaking, but it has allowed the National Planning Department (DNP in Spanish), the government's main planning entity, to evaluate the country's progress in the fight against poverty. In fact, the LCI is included in the national development plans prepared by the

[9] See CEPAL (2001, 2007) and Feres and Mancero (2002).
[10] See DANE (1989), Izaguirre Corzo (2007), and Fresneda Bautista (2007).
[11] The Social Mission of the National Planning Department developed the LCI. It has a scale of 1 to 100, in which a higher score means better living conditions in aspects such as housing, infrastructure, social capital, and education (Sarmiento and Ramírez, 1997).

DNP, which steer the course for each administration in its respective term. The LCI, rather than an indicator of multidimensional poverty, is an indicator of multidimensional well-being. Due to this characteristic—its multidimensional nature—it created a fertile ground of data collection and analysis for introducing the MPI in the country.

Finally, we had a System for the Identification of Potential Social Program Beneficiaries, known as the SISBEN. This system was created in President Ernesto Samper's administration (1994–1998), and its goal since then has been to objectively identify people living in poverty and vulnerable situations in order to ensure that social investment reaches those most in need. It is based on household surveys, carried out in person, which are used to assign a score to each family according to their living conditions. Families with low scores automatically become beneficiaries of all available public assistance programs and benefits.[12] It is another multidimensional social policy instrument that was designed, precisely, based on the LCI. Nevertheless, this very important instrument must be cleaned up because it is also being fraudulently used by people who are not living in poverty.

At the end of the 2010s, the UBN Index and the LCI helped to characterize poverty and target social policies, while the SISBEN determined which households were potential beneficiaries. All these processes entailed—and this is very important—multidimensional assessments. With respect to a standard poverty measure, we had only one: the traditional monetary or income poverty measure based on objective income criteria set by the World Bank.[13] This measure was first implemented in Colombia in 1987, and it has been updated several times since then (Cepeda et al., 2018). The last time was in 2020.

I must say—with a dose of patriotic pride, but also undoubtedly grounded in reality—that at least three factors come together in Colombia to positively influence the development of our economic and social policies. First, we have highly qualified human capital. I am referring specifically to our serious and dedicated economists, from excellent academic backgrounds, who work with the government or industry associations. Second, historically, we have maintained a tradition of reliability and compliance in our economic performance that has earned us the international community's respect. Without exception, we have strictly honored the payment of our obligations to multilateral

---

[12] Using a questionnaire that applicants must fill out, a series of data is processed and analyzed to assign a score. The purpose of the score is to target social program beneficiaries in areas such as health, education, and social well-being (SISBEN, 2020).

[13] According to World Bank standards, in a country such as Colombia, which is part of the upper-middle income group, a person is considered to be in poverty if they live on less than $5.50 per day. They are considered to be in extreme poverty if they live on less than $1.90 per day (World Bank, 2014).

financial institutions and banks, a fact setting us apart in Latin America, and we have avoided situations of hyperinflation such as those that have affected many countries in the region. And third, in the economic sphere, we have public entities that act with professionalism and objectivity and that are above political whims. In particular, these entities include the Central Bank and its board of directors, which independently guides the country's monetary policy, and the DNP, a ministerial-level institution that coordinates the country's short-, medium-, and long-term planning according to strictly technical criteria, as well as the prioritization of our investment resources.

Our economists at the DNP, used to working with the UBN Index, the LCI, the SISBEN, and the income poverty measure in their work to plan and target investments, soon discovered that there was a new and more comprehensive indicator beginning to make its way around the academic world: the MPI.

A group of economists at the DNP eagerly read Alkire and Foster's working paper in 2008, shortly after its publication. They were also aware of the multidimensional poverty measure being developed in Mexico by CONEVAL. The analysts had been using the UBN Index, the LCI, and the SISBEN, but they were aware that only the first served to evaluate poverty multidimensionally, while the latter two were indicators of well-being or living standards that could be indirectly useful for measuring poverty. Although the UBN Index and the LCI had multidimensional characteristics, the analysts understood that their thematic content had, in their own words, also "lost relevance" and proved to be "insufficient" (Angulo et al., 2011, p. 5).

Thus, at the Colombian government's most important technical planning entity, the ground was more than fertile for studying and analyzing possible MPI implementation. A crisis with the calculation of the monetary poverty index and decisive political will would be responsible for turning this possibility into a reality.

The Best Opportunities Emerge from Crises

I believe in that old proverb, attributed to ancient Chinese wisdom, which invites us to discover the opportunities behind every crisis. In the case of the MPI's emergence in Colombia, this proverb turned out to be right.

As mentioned above, the main method for measuring poverty in Colombia, as well as in most countries in the world, was the monetary or income poverty method based on the World Bank's guidelines. In 2006, the DANE changed the household survey methodology used to obtain the poverty indicator without conducting a parallel survey to validate it. This produced a statistics crisis due to the loss of comparability in the poverty series—and not only that series but also the employment and inequality series. The problem was so huge that practically two years of data—2006 and 2007—were lost as they could not be compared with previous years. As can be imagined, this damaged the credibility of the statistics and social achievements of my predecessor Álvaro Uribe's administration. At the time, I was the minister of defense and was focused on coordinating the State's response to guerrilla groups, criminal gangs, and drug-trafficking mafias. This crisis was never discussed in the Cabinet.

The truth is that the Colombian economy had demonstrated strong growth in 2006 and 2007, and poverty had also decreased. The lack of reliable data to demonstrate that decrease was unfortunate, but this was the crisis needed to produce a revolutionary change in measuring poverty.

In early 2009, the government convened a mission of experts, called the Mission for the Splicing of Employment, Poverty, and Inequality Series (MESEP in Spanish), to definitively resolve this issue. Some of the best economists in the country took part, with contributions from experts at ECLAC and the World Bank, who were joined by the DANE and DNP teams. Roberto Angulo, an economist from the Universidad Javeriana, served as the MESEP's technical secretary. I highlight Angulo's participation because later on, as the DNP's deputy director of social promotion and quality of life, he would participate—together with Yadira Díaz and Renata Pardo—in the design and implementation of the Colombian MPI.[14]

The people who came together in the MESEP were a true dream team, with members performing their work free of charge and with the greatest enthusiasm. Their first task, which they carried out between January and September 2009, was to recover the comparability of the poverty series, a labor of statistical archaeology. A second phase of work, much more future-oriented, lasted for two years from September 2009 to August 2011. It was focused on designing a new methodology to measure monetary poverty and a proposal for an institutional agreement to estimate poverty figures. The MESEP, ultimately, would be the group to recommend adopting the MPI.

A very interesting debate emerged about accounting for in-kind and cash benefits and assistance to the most vulnerable people in the calculation of monetary poverty. International good practices—such as those promoted by ECLAC, for example—indicate that only cash transfers, not in-kind assistance, should be included. However, this makes it difficult to monitor social policies' effect on poverty. For example, if education coverage is doubled or

---

[14] For more on MESEP, see DNP and DANE (2012).

early childhood care for the lowest-income population is increased, this is indeed indisputable progress in quality of life, but it may not be reflected in increased income for one or two generations. With the exception of cash transfers, other social programs are not reflected in, and have no real-time impact on, monetary poverty rates.

This debate motivated the DNP economists to begin researching the possibility of having an MPI similar to the one being developed in Mexico but using the methodology that was becoming known in the academic world due to the work of professors Alkire and Foster and the recently established OPHI.

The crisis in the 2006 and 2007 poverty series thus helped to generate momentum for a change in the poverty measure in Colombia—a change that would be defined and consolidated a few years later, during my administration.

A chance encounter would help accelerate the winds of change. On March 11, 2010, President Uribe, who had less than five months left in office, traveled to Santiago, Chile, to attend the presidential inauguration of Sebastián Piñera. He traveled with his communications advisor, Mauricio Carradini, who met a good Bolivian friend of his, Diego Zavaleta, during the swearing-in ceremony. At the time, Zavaleta was working as a researcher at OPHI and was tasked with promoting and supporting the implementation of multidimensional poverty measures in several countries. Zavaleta, with a doctorate in development studies from the University of Oxford, was destined to play a leading role in the construction of the Colombian MPI.

Carradini told the president about the multidimensional measure that Zavaleta was promoting. Uribe invited him to get on the presidential plane and fly with them to Bogotá, so that Zavaleta could tell him about it and make contact with the DNP experts who were seeking innovative solutions to better measure poverty.

As soon as Zavaleta arrived in Bogotá, he met with the DNP team led by Roberto Angulo. It was a providential meeting. They began a joint working group that same day and started sharing their knowledge and experiences. Zavaleta was very impressed by the exercises based on the Alkire–Foster method that the Colombian economists had carried out on their own initiative.

Two months later, in May 2010, a seminar organized by ECLAC and OPHI on multidimensional poverty measurement in Latin America was held in Santiago, Chile. The three staff members in charge of this subject at the DNP attended. There, they met Sabina Alkire and James Foster, as well as John Hammock, the other co-founder of OPHI, together with Professor Alkire.[15]

---

[15] A brief report on this seminar may be found in ECLAC (2010).

The DNP experts and the OPHI leaders developed a warm relationship, and it was there, in ECLAC's formal meeting room, that they decided to expedite their cooperation to design the Colombian MPI (C-MPI).

Months of intense work followed, with weekly videoconferences between the DNP and OPHI. OPHI's contributions in communications strategy, statistical management, and rigorous calculations complemented the Colombian economists' studies and technical capacity. However, the initial goal of having a C-MPI before the end of the Uribe administration was not reached.

On July 20, 2010, when I had already been elected as his successor, President Uribe gave his last speech reporting back to Congress. In it, he affirmed that "poverty is not only a lack of income," and he mentioned the existence of the global MPI launched by OPHI (Uribe, 2010).

In his speech, he cited a provisional calculation made by the DNP, which still needed several adjustments. The figure he mentioned—about a 9% multidimensional poverty rate in Colombia—turned out to be quite far from reality. The outgoing president mentioned this percentage, which could hold validity in the context of Latin America but did not account for other DNP variables that would result in a multidimensional poverty rate of at least 26%.[16]

Despite this initial inaccuracy, the truth is that even if momentum for a multidimensional measure was already building, commitment and political will from the new administration were required not only to adopt the MPI but also to make it into an effective public policy tool against poverty. And that—commitment and political will—was what we had.

C-MPI Discussion Begins

I was only five days away from being inaugurated as president of Colombia when an academic seminar took place in Bogotá at the Universidad EAFIT campus. It included a preliminary presentation of progress on C-MPI design.

Held on August 2, 2010, the seminar was titled "Human Opportunities and the Measurement of Poverty in Colombia." Attendees included Sabina Alkire, James Foster, and other OPHI researchers; Gonzalo Hernández, executive secretary of Mexico's CONEVAL; and the MESEP experts. There, the advantages and disadvantages of the new index proposed by the DNP were put to the test in an open debate.

---

[16] These figures were discussed in a debate on the new poverty measurement with scholars and DNP staff members in August 2010 (EAFIT, 2010).

According to the DNP's presentation at the seminar, the department considered it necessary to build a new index, including the following characteristics:

1. Complements the income poverty measure (before and after benefits) and includes a dashboard for the measurement of living conditions.
2. Takes into account a multidimensional notion of poverty.
3. Allows comparisons among population groups in terms of variables susceptible to modification through public policy.
4. Expresses losses and gains in specific dimensions within the population living in poverty.
5. Is specific to the Colombian context.
6. Measures not only the incidence of poverty but also the poverty gap and the severity of poverty (this synthesizes the above needs).

(Angulo, 2010)

The event was a success, and it revealed the technical and very professional way in which Colombians were handling the process to design the new poverty measure. Similar to that first encounter in Santiago, Chile, this meeting between the DNP experts and OPHI founders and leaders led to tremendous progress in designing and implementing the C-MPI.

Lesson 1
Poverty Is Much More Than a Lack of Income

Professor Amartya Sen makes a distinction between the "direct method" for measuring poverty, based on determining whether people meet or do not meet their basic needs, and the "income method," which establishes a minimum income above which it is assumed that all basic needs are met. Sen is clear in stating that the direct method is superior to the income method because it is not based on assumptions and because it shows, to a greater extent, whether people are or are not living in decent conditions. He explains it in his book *Poverty and Famines* as follows:

In identifying the poor for a given set of "basic needs", it is possible to use at least two alternative methods. One is simply to check the set of people whose actual consumption baskets happen to leave some basic need unsatisfied. This we may call the "direct method", and it does not involve the use of any income notion, in particular not that of a poverty-line income. In contrast, in what may be called the "income method", the first step is to calculate the minimum income at which all the specified minimum needs are satisfied. The next step is to identify those whose actual incomes fall below that poverty line.

In an obvious sense the direct method is superior to the income method, since the former is not based on particular assumptions of consumption behaviour which may or may not be accurate. Indeed, it could be argued that only in the absence of direct information regarding the satisfaction of the specified needs can there be a case for bringing in the intermediary of income, so that the income method is at most a second best.

(Sen, 1981, p. 26)

This reflection by Professor Sen revolutionized the way of measuring and considering poverty, which until then was almost exclusively based on the one-dimensional criterion of people's monetary income. An economist or statistician's work consisted of determining how much income was required for a person to satisfy their basic needs. Thus, the equation was solved: if a person makes less than that value (the so-called poverty line), they are poor; if they make more than it, they are not.

But the truth is that poverty is much more than a lack of economic resources; its reality is more complex and goes beyond a number. Two families with the same income level may have very different living conditions, depending on their environment, their ability to work, their access to education and health services, their housing quality, or their access to basic utility services such as drinking water and electricity. The mere fact that one family lives in a house with a tiled floor and the other in a house with a dirt floor or that one family cooks on a wood stove and the other on a gas or electric stove makes a fundamental difference, even if they have the same income. This vision led Professor Sen to conclude that a multidimensional poverty indicator was necessary.

For a government, responsible for deciding the amount and allocation of social investment, it is much more useful to understand and measure poverty in its various dimensions beyond income. This enables advancing policies and programs that focus on the most pressing deprivations and on the conditions that most affect the most vulnerable people's quality of life.

References

Alkire, S. (1995). "The full or minimally decent life: Empiricization of Sen's capabilities approach in poverty measurement" [Master's thesis]. University of Oxford.

Alkire, S. (1998). "Operationalizing Amartya Sen's capability approach to human development: A framework for identifying valuable capabilities" [DPhil thesis]. University of Oxford.

Alkire, S., and Foster, J. (2007). "Counting and multidimensional poverty measurement." Oxford Poverty and Human Development Initiative (OPHI), OPHI Working Paper 7.

Alkire, S., and Foster, J. (2011). "Counting and multidimensional poverty measurement." *Journal of Public Economics*, *95*(7), 476–487. https://doi.org/10.1016/j.jpubeco.2010.11.006.

Alkire, S., and Seth, S. (2013). "Selecting a targeting method to identify BPL households in India." *Social Indicators Research*, *112*(2), 417–446. https://doi.org/10.1007/s11205-013-0254-6.

Altimir, O. (1982). "The extent of poverty in Latin America." World Bank Group, World Bank Staff Working Papers No. SWP 522, July 1. http://documents.worldbank.org/curated/en/187461468743796622/The-extent-of-poverty-in-Latin-America.

Angulo, R. (2010). "Propuesta de un Índice de Pobreza Multidimensional (IPM-OPHI) para Colombia" [PowerPoint slides]. Departamento Nacional de Planeación, Archivos de Economía No. 382, October 5. https://economia.uniandes.edu.co/sites/default/files/seminariocede/IPM-Colombia-300910-Seminario-CEDE-.pdf.

Angulo, R., Díaz, Y., and Pardo, R. (2011). "Índice de Pobreza Multidimensional para Colombia (IPM-Colombia) 1997–2010." Departamento Nacional de Planeación, November 8. https://colaboracion.dnp.gov.co/cdt/estudios%20econmicos/382.pdf.

Azevedo, V., and Robles, M. (2013). "Multidimensional targeting: Identifying beneficiaries of conditional cash transfer programs." *Social Indicators Research*, *112*(2), 447–475. https://doi.org/10.1007/s11205-013-0255-5.

Batana, Y. (2013). "Multidimensional measurement of poverty among women in Sub-Saharan Africa." *Social Indicators Research*, *112*(2), 337–362. https://doi.org/10.1007/s11205-013-0251-9.

Battiston, D., Cruces, G., López-Calva, L. F., Lugo, M. A., and Santos, M. E. (2013). "Income and beyond: Multidimensional poverty in six Latin American countries." *Social Indicators Research*, *112*(2), 291–314. https://doi.org/10.1007/s11205-013-0249-3.

CEPAL (Economic Commission for Latin America and the Caribbean). (2001). "El método de las necesidades básicas insatisfechas (NBI) y sus aplicaciones en América Latina." February. https://www.cepal.org/es/publicaciones/4784-metodo-necesidades-basicas-insatisfechas-nbi-sus-aplicaciones-america-latina.

CEPAL. (2007). "La medida de necesidades básicas insatisfechas (NBI) como instrumento de medición de la pobreza y focalización de programas." November. https://www.cepal.org/es/publicaciones/4816-la-medida-necesidades-basicas-insatisfechas-nbi-como-instrumento-medicion-la.

Cepeda, L., Ocampo, R., Rivas, G., Álvarez, S., Rodríguez, R., Álvarez, L., and Zambrano, E. (2018). "Pobreza monetaria y pobreza multidimensional: Análisis 2010–2017." Departamento Nacional de Planeación, July. https://colaboracion.dnp.gov.co/CDT/Desarrollo%20Social/Pobreza%20Monetaria%20y%20Multidimensional%20en%20Colombia%202010-2017.pdf.

Chen, H., and Zhang, Q. H. (2013). "Urban multidimensional poverty measurement based on the Alkire–Foster model: A case study of Zhongshan City." *Journal of Wuyi University (Natural Sciences Edition), 27*(2), 32–36.

CONEVAL (National Council for the Evaluation of Social Development Policy). (2018). "Medición de la pobreza. Lineamientos y criterios para la definición, identificación, y medición de la pobreza." https://www.coneval.org.mx/Medicion/MP/Paginas/Lineamientos_DOF.aspx.

CONEVAL. (2019). "Metodología para la medición multidimensional de la pobreza" (3rd edn). https://www.coneval.org.mx/InformesPublicaciones/InformesPublicaciones/Documents/Metodologia-medicion-multidimensional-3er-edicion.pdf.

DANE (National Administrative Department of Statistics). (1989). La pobreza en Colombia, tomo I. DANE.

DNP (National Planning Department), and DANE. (2012). "Misión para el Empalme de las Series de Empleo, Pobreza y Desigualdad (MESEP). Pobreza monetaria en Colombia: Nueva metodología y cifras 2002–2010." https://www.dane.gov.co/files/noticias/Pobreza_nuevametodologia.pdf.

Drèze, J., and Sen, A. (1989). *Hunger and public action*. Clarendon Press.

Drèze, J., and Sen, A. (1995). *India: Economic development and social opportunity*. Oxford University Press.

Duclos, J. Y., Sahn, D. E., and Younger, S. D. (2008). "Using an ordinal approach to multidimensional poverty analysis." In N. Kakwani and J. Silber (eds), *Quantitative approaches to multidimensional poverty measurement* (pp. 244–261). Palgrave Macmillan.

EAFIT. (2010). "Debate sobre la pobreza, desde indicadores y dimensiones." Universidad EAFIT, August 4. http://www.eafit.edu.co/agencia-noticias/historico-

noticias/2010/agosto/Paginas/debate-pobreza-indicadores-dimensiones.
aspx.

ECLAC (Economic Commission for Latin America and the Caribbean). (2010). "Prioritizing equality and redefining poverty is imperative for a new development model." May 13. https://www.cepal.org/en/pressreleases/prioritizing-equality-and-redefining-poverty-imperative-new-development-model.

Feres, J. C., and Mancero, X. (2002). "El método de las necesidades básicas insatisfechas (NBI) y sus aplicaciones en América Latina." CEPAL, February. https://www.cepal.org/es/publicaciones/4784-metodo-necesidades-basicas-insatisfechas-nbi-sus-aplicaciones-america-latina.

Foster, J., Greer, J., and Thorbecke, E. (1984). "A class of decomposable poverty measures." *Econometrica*, 52(3), 761–766. https://doi.org/10.2307/1913475.

Fresneda Bautista, O. (2007). "La medida de necesidades básicas insatisfechas (NBI) como instrumento de medición de la pobreza y focalización de programas." CEPAL, November. https://www.cepal.org/es/publicaciones/4816-la-medida-necesidades-basicas-insatisfechas-nbi-como-instrumento-medicion-la.

Izaguirre Corzo, A. C. (2007). Mapas de pobreza para México: 2005. Instituto Tecnológica y de Estudios Superiores de Monterrey, Campus Ciudad de México. Escuela de Graduados en Administración Pública.

Ley General de Desarrollo Social. (2018). "Texto vigente. Últimas reformas publicadas." DOF, June 25. https://www.coneval.org.mx/Evaluacion/NME/Documents/Ley_General_de_Desarrollo_Social.pdf.

Mitra, S. (2013). "Towards a multidimensional measure of governance." *Social Indicators Research*, 112(2), 477–496. https://doi.org/10.1007/s11205-013-0256-4.

Multidimensional Poverty Peer Network (MPPN). (2016). "Gonzalo Hernández Licona: 'In Mexico, social policy has focused on multidimensional measurement.'" *Dimensions*, November 4. https://mppn.org/hernandez-licona-entrevista.

National Statistics Bureau, Royal Government of Bhutan. (2013). "Bhutan Multidimensional Poverty Index 2012." http://202.144.146.196/publication/files/pub0ll1571bt.pdf.

National Statistics Bureau, Royal Government of Bhutan, and OPHI (Oxford Poverty and Human Development Initiative). (2017). "Multidimensional Poverty Index 2017." https://ophi.org.uk/wp-content/uploads/Bhutan_2017_vs5_23Dec_online.pdf.

Roche, J. M. (2013). "Monitoring progress in child poverty reduction: Methodological insights and illustration to the case study of Bangladesh." *Social Indicators Research*, 112(2), 363–390. https://doi.org/10.1007/s11205-013-0252-8.

Roelen, K., and Camfield, L. (2013). "A mixed-method taxonomy of child poverty—the case of Ethiopia." *Applied Research in Quality of Life*, 8(3), 319–337. https://doi.org/10.1007/s11482-012-9195-5.

Santos, M. E. (2013). "Tracking poverty reduction in Bhutan: Income deprivation alongside deprivation in other sources of happiness." *Social Indicators Research*, 112(2), 259–290. https://doi.org/10.1007/s11205-013-0248-4.

Santos, M. E., and Ura, K. (2008). "Multidimensional poverty in Bhutan: Estimates and policy implications." University of Oxford, OPHI Working Paper No. 14, September. https://ophi.org.uk/working-paper-number-14.

Sarmiento, A., and Ramírez, C. (1997). "El índice de condiciones de vida." Planeación y Desarrollo, 28(1), 200–230. https://colaboracion.dnp.gov.co/CDT/RevistaPD/1997/pd_vXXVIII_n1_1997_art.7.pdf

Sen, A. (1976). "Poverty: An ordinal approach to measurement." *Econometrica*, 44(2), 219–231. https://doi.org/10.2307/1912718.

Sen, A. (1978). "Three notes on the concept of poverty." International Labor Organization, ILO Working Papers No. 991757103402676.

Sen, A. (1979). "Informational analysis of moral principles." In R. Harrison (ed.), *Rational action* (pp. 115–132). Cambridge University Press.

Sen, A. (1981). *Poverty and famines: An essay on entitlement and deprivation.* Clarendon Press.

Sen, A. (1985). "Well-being, agency and freedom: The Dewey Lectures 1984." *Journal of Philosophy*, 82(4), 169–221. https://doi.org/10.2307/2026184.

Sen, A. (1987). *On ethics and economics.* Basil Blackwell.

Sen, A. (1990). "Development as capability expansion." In K. Griffin and J. Knight (eds), *Human development and the international development strategy for the 1990s* (pp. 41–58). MacMillan.

Sen, A. (1991). "Welfare, preference and freedom." *Journal of Econometrics*, 50, 15–29. https://doi.org/10.1016/0304-4076(91)90087-T.

Sen, A. (1992). *Inequality reexamined.* Harvard University Press.

Sen, A. (1993). "Capability and well-being." In A. Sen and M. Nussbaum (eds.), *The quality of life* (pp. 30–53). Clarendon Press.

SISBEN (System for the Identification of Potential Social Program Beneficiaries). (2020). "Sisbén: Sistema de selección de beneficiarios para programas sociales." https://consultarsisben.com.

Trani, J.-F., Biggeri, M., and Mauro, V. (2013). "The multidimensionality of child poverty: Evidence from Afghanistan." *Social Indicators Research*, 112(2), 391–416. https://doi.org/10.1007/s11205-013-0253-7.

Ura, K., Alkire, S., Zangmo, T., and Wangdi, K. (2012). "An extensive analysis of the Gross National Happiness Index." Centre for Bhutan Studies. https://opendocs.ids.ac.uk/opendocs/handle/20.500.12413/11818.

Ura, K., Alkire, S., Zangmo, T., and Wangdi, K. (2015). *Preliminary analysis of the Gross National Happiness Index 2015.* Centre for Bhutan Studies.

Uribe, A. (2010, July 19). "Discurso completo del presidente Álvaro Uribe." *Semana*, July 19. https://www.semana.com/politica/articulo/discurso-completo-del-presidente-alvaro-uribe/119536-3.

World Bank. (2014). "Colombia policy notes: Toward sustainable peace, poverty eradication and shared prosperity." September. https://www.worldbank.org/content/dam/Worldbank/Feature%20Story/lac/Colombia%20Policy%20Notes%20Finalweb%20%20Sept%2024-2014.pdf.

Yu, J. (2013). "Multidimensional poverty in China: Findings based on the CHNS." *Social Indicators Research*, *112*(2), 315–336. https://doi.org/10.1007/s11205-013-0250-x.

2
Colombia

A Pioneer in MPI Adoption

Beyond the "Adam Complex"

I am convinced that every new administration should pick up and continue its predecessor's positive initiatives and programs, correct or improve them as necessary, and propose new programs and policies that leave a personal stamp. In other words, it shouldn't start from scratch, as if nothing from the past were worthwhile, but rather build on and improve what has already been built.

Many government leaders have a terrible habit, particularly rooted in Latin America, which is often called the "Adam complex." It consists of undervaluing and tossing out everything that previous administrations have achieved, expecting history to begin with the new administration as if the new leader were Adam, the first man on Earth. How much time, how many resources have been lost due to leaders' arrogant attempts to avoid following in their predecessors' footsteps, even when these footsteps make sense and are headed in the right direction?

In my case, I continued and improved very important social initiatives, policies, and programs from previous administrations. That was precisely what happened with the Colombian Multidimensional Poverty Index (C-MPI). When I took office as president on August 7, 2010, I found work on the index well underway—even though it was still in the experimental phase, with no official document or regulation adopting it. I saw that it was promising and decided to continue with the same team of technical experts who were working on its design.

As mentioned in the Introduction, in my presidential campaign, I had declared the fight against poverty to be one of my priorities, alongside ending an internal war that spread not only death and pain but also destitution in our territory. With this in mind, I appointed Samuel Azout, an economist from Cornell University and a successful businessman from Colombia's Caribbean region, as senior advisor for social prosperity. I knew about Azout's effectiveness, as well as his social sensitivity, and so I put him in charge of this office

The Battle Against Poverty. Juan Manuel Santos, Oxford University Press. © Juan Manuel Santos (2023). DOI: 10.1093/oso/9780192885234.003.0003

with clear instructions to coordinate everything with the National Planning Department (DNP in Spanish).

I appointed the economist Hernando José Gómez to lead the DNP. He had been the co-director of Colombia's central bank and successfully negotiated our country's free trade agreement with the United States. Gómez, holding a PhD in economics from Yale University, was impressed, as Azout had been, by the virtues of the new poverty index that the DNP was working on with technical support from the Oxford Poverty and Human Development Initiative (OPHI). Therefore, he retained the group of economists who had been leading the work so far.

When they spoke to me in more detail about the C-MPI that was being designed, I understood even more clearly this instrument's enormous potential for advancing one of my administration's main priorities: the fight against poverty. To learn first-hand about their work, I asked them to bring the team of technical experts to the Office of the President. The meeting lasted approximately an hour-and-a-half, and María Lorena Gutiérrez, senior advisor for good governance, also participated. María Lorena, who holds a PhD in business administration from Tulane University, had been the dean of the Business Administration Faculty at the Universidad de los Andes, and she became one of my most trusted officials. Her work to coordinate the crusade to reduce poverty in our country was essential.

In the meeting, the DNP experts explained in detail the philosophy and advantages of having an MPI in Colombia as a poverty measure complementing the monetary income-based measure we had been using. They also showed me a project with a dashboard, in which a user could select various dimensions of poverty and assess progress on them. As an economist and government leader, I was fascinated by this new index that reflected the teachings of my professor Amartya Sen. I saw that it was a clear, clean, summary indicator, an indicator that communicated and, at the same time, served to help target and optimize the government's social investment. I became its most enthusiastic advocate.

I remember calling Professor Sen, who was in Boston, and telling him about my interest in this index that had been developed based on his theories. He was very pleased and recommended that I contact OPHI and, in particular, the creators of the Alkire–Foster methodology, which I did. A couple of years later, on June 6, 2013, at the invitation of Dr Alkire, I had the happy opportunity to meet my former professor again, at an event at the University of Oxford: the launch of the Multidimensional Poverty Peer Network (MPPN). There, I gave a speech about the way we were implementing the MPI in Colombia and our first and very promising results in the fight against poverty and inequality. It was immensely satisfying for me to share with my former teacher the start of a global network of countries that are developing, using, or exploring this innovative measurement. Eventually, in May 2018, both Professor Sen and I were appointed co-founders of the MPPN, which was a great honor for me.

C-MPI Inclusion in the National Development Plan

Proposed by each administration in its first months, the National Development Plan steers the course for each administration's priorities, pursued objectives, and investment resources allocated to fulfilling these objectives. It is a technical yet also programmatic document, which the DNP, as the country's main planning entity, is in charge of preparing and coordinating. It is discussed in the Cabinet and, ultimately, Congress approves it. It then becomes a national law.

During my presidential campaign, I made "democratic prosperity" the defining characteristic of my administration, so it was not difficult to establish the title of the National Development Plan for my first term (2010–2014). It was called "Prosperity for All," and it focused on the objectives of reducing poverty and seeking greater equity in a country that, sadly, was competing with Haiti for the title of most unequal country in the Western Hemisphere.

As Angulo and Zavaleta (2018, p. 17) recall, as incoming president, my instructions to my staff were summarized in two particular tasks: (1) ensuring that my administration's National Development Plan would have "an important and explicit emphasis on reducing poverty and inequality" and (2) designing "good governance management tools that would help [. . .] monitor results in order to concretely verify outcomes."

Coordinated by the DNP, and together with my team of advisors at the Office of the President, we began to draft the National Development Plan and define a very important component: the targets, which put a specific number on the objectives in various areas of national life that we aimed to meet. It soon became clear that this new poverty index the DNP was working on with support from OPHI, which included 5 dimensions and 15 indicators, would be very useful for monitoring our progress on the issue of equal opportunities.

Consequently, we decided to incorporate the recently constructed C-MPI into the National Development Plan's targets. We did so with a very ambitious goal: to reduce the C-MPI baseline of 34.6% in 2009 to 22.4% in 2014 (DNP, 2010, p. 64).

It was the first time that a country had included the MPI in its development plan as a strategic indicator of its management.

To achieve this, the DNP took a very important step. While preparing a development plan, it typically created microsimulation models to set a monetary poverty reduction target. In other words, based on the targets proposed by various ministries, the DNP would calculate how they affected the anticipated monetary poverty outcome. Even without the C-MPI calculation methodology being officially adopted, the DNP team carried out the same microsimulation work with this index. They took the targets sector by sector—housing, health, education, basic utility services coverage—and ran programs to simulate public policy scenarios using microdata from the National Quality of Life Survey (ECV in Spanish). That's how they set a C-MPI target that the government could commit to for 2014.[1]

I vividly remember a meeting we had in my office, in which Hernando José Gómez and other DNP staff members presented this work to me. In a single slide, they summarized how the National Development Plan's sector targets impacted multidimensional poverty. The equation was, more or less, the following: *if the NDP's sector targets are met and if all ministers fulfill their four-year commitments, multidimensional poverty will drop from A to B, and the investment required to achieve this will be C.*

On that day, I understood that the C-MPI's virtues went beyond being an indicator that included several dimensions of poverty and beyond its usefulness to target programs and social investment. It was also an extraordinary governance tool that made it possible to assess and monitor the various ministries' sectoral progress and determine whether or not they contributed to the higher goal of reducing poverty. This index, with its capacity for synthesis, would allow us to tie sectoral policies to a national objective, while at the same time determining the amount of resources to allocate to it.[2]

I gave clear instructions: "We need to create a special high-level roundtable [3] that should meet regularly to evaluate our progress in the fight against poverty, as well as a dashboard that cleanly and clearly indicates how we are doing on meeting our social goals." I wanted the entire government to concentrate and focus, as if it were one person, on the goal of poverty reduction.

---

[1] For more information on how these simulations were performed, see Angulo and Zavaleta (2018, pp. 17–20).

[2] Angulo (2016) illustrates how, in the case of Colombia, the MPI has been used to organize the institutional architecture and to establish a budget. Another more recent case is that of Costa Rica, where the national budget is organized and prioritized according to national MPI results (Costa Rica Gobierno del Bicentenario, Ministerio de Planificación Nacional y Política Economica, and Ministerio de Hacienda Costa Rica, 2019).

[3] Chapter 4 will elaborate on the establishment and operations of this cross-cutting roundtable for monitoring social policies to combat poverty.

On June 16, 2011, I signed Law 1450, issuing the 2010–2014 National Development Plan, "Prosperity for All" (Congreso de la República, 2011). Just over two months later, we officially introduced the C-MPI to Colombia and the world.

C-MPI Calculation and Characteristics

When we adopted the C-MPI, two things were very clear. First, this new indicator had to evaluate different dimensions that produce poverty in a household, these dimensions had to be representative, and we had to have measurable and verifiable data that would make up the index. Second, and this is very important, we decided that the C-MPI's adoption did not in any way mean abolishing the monetary income poverty measure that had been in use. These two measures are complementary and not mutually exclusive: each one provides us with a different but very valid picture of poverty in the country. In addition, we did not want to create suspicion that we had changed the poverty measure for political purposes, to show better results with a new index. If we wanted to preserve the credibility of our social indicators, we had to keep the monetary poverty index and complement it with the C-MPI. We did just that, and both indices have continued to be used since then.[4]

This means that, in Colombia, since 2011, we have two official poverty measures that, in some way, correspond to the classification proposed by Amartya Sen in 1981.[5] On the one hand is the direct measure, the C-MPI, which evaluates people's degree of satisfaction with respect to living conditions such as health, education, employment, and housing. On the other hand is the monetary poverty measure or indirect measure, which evaluates a household's ability to acquire goods and services based on a defined minimum income, below which a household is considered to be living in poverty or extreme poverty.

It was a fortunate coincidence that the new multidimensional poverty indicator was designed at the same time as the 2010–2014 National Development Plan. The C-MPI was established at a time of defining public policies, for which its calculation and projections were crucial.

The key to an MPI is precisely its multidimensional nature, and therefore selecting the dimensions or variables of poverty included in its calculation is

---

[4] DNP studies (2017) show the complementary nature and advantages of having both monetary and multidimensional poverty indicators in Colombia. These indicators have also been jointly analyzed in other countries such as Uganda (Gaddis and Klasen, 2012), Germany (Suppa, 2016), and the Sub-Saharan Africa region (Salecker et al., 2020).

[5] Amartya Sen delves into this aspect in Sen (1997, 1999).

essential to its design and implementation. In our case, we defined 5 dimensions, broken down into 15 indicators according to certain defined criteria. The experts in charge of designing the C-MPI summarize it as follows:

> The following elements were considered in the definition of dimensions, indicators, and cut-off points for the C-MPI:
>
> — A review of frequently used variables from other indices applied in Latin America
> — The Political Constitution of Colombia
> — A review of the literature on priority dimensions and variables often used in multidimensional indices applied to Colombia (Unsatisfied Basic Needs, Living Conditions Index, SISBEN III)
> — Direct relationship with the national government's social policy
> — Voices of the Poor studies in Colombia
> — The thresholds set by the Millennium Development Goals (MDGs Colombia) and by the respective sectoral policies
> — The availability of data within a single statistical source (the DANE's [National Administrative Department of Statistics'] Quality of Life Survey)
> — Discussions with experts and sector heads.
>
> (Angulo et al., 2011, p. 14)

Based on this process, five dimensions were defined: household education conditions, conditions of children and youth, employment, health, and access to public utilities and housing conditions. These dimensions are measured using 15 indicators:

Table 2.1 C-MPI dimensions and indicators

Dimension	Indicator
I. Household education conditions	1. Educational achievement (among people aged 15 or older)
	2. Literacy (among people aged 15 or older)
II. Conditions of children and youth	3. School attendance (among children aged 6–16)
	4. No school lag (among children aged 7–17)
	5. Access to early childhood care services (among children aged 0–5)
	6. No child labor (among children aged 12–17)
III. Employment	7. No long-term unemployment

Continued

Dimension	Indicator
	8. Formal employment
IV. Health	9. Health insurance coverage
	10. Access to health services in case of need
V. Access to public utilities and housing conditions	11. Access to an improved water source
	12. Adequate elimination of sewer waste
	13. Adequate floors
	14. Adequate external walls
	15. No critical overcrowding

Source: Based on Angulo and Zavaleta (2018).

Satisfaction of the included dimensions is essential for what we might call a dignified life, but other dimensions could also be included. These dimensions and indicators were chosen because the methodology requires all variables to come from the same source, and the best source we currently have in Colombia is the ECV conducted by the DANE.[6] This does not prevent, if necessary, broadening the information this survey collects in the future and thus including new dimensions or indicators in the C-MPI calculation.[7]

It is clear that an index based on considering these elements is much more comprehensive and says much more about a household's condition than an index solely based on a criterion of monetary income. A family group in Colombia made up of four people (father, mother, and two children) may have, together, an income greater than one million Colombian pesos per month (around 216 dollars), meaning they are not poor according to the income criterion (DANE, 2019a). However, they may be living in conditions that suggest a situation of poverty—for example, with no health insurance, far from any health center, no access to water, in a house with dirt floors, or in overcrowded conditions.

What is the C-MPI poverty line? We found that, on average, households that identify themselves as poor experience deprivations in at least one-third of the 15 indicators that form the basis of the index. Consequently, we decided to make this value—one-third of the 15 possible deprivations—the threshold to determine who is living in multidimensional poverty (Angulo, 2011).

It is important to note that, to calculate the C-MPI, the unit of analysis is the household, not the individual. This makes sense because all people within

[6] At the end of the 1980s, available indices included the Unsatisfied Basic Needs Index and the poverty line. In order to capture other dimensions not present in these, the Quality of Life Survey was designed. It was initially applied in Bogotá in 1991 and then nationally in 1993. Since then, methodological changes have been made to improve the coverage and quality of the collected data. It was conducted annually from 2010 to 2018 (DANE, 2019a).

[7] Alkire and Foster (2007) reflect on the dimensions missing from the multidimensional poverty measure.

a household experience the same deprivations. Additionally, the fact that measuring poverty by household encourages union and supportive bonds among family members was taken into account.

Adoption of the C-MPI

I completed my first year as president on August 7, 2011. This date coincided with the Mission for the Splicing of Employment, Poverty, and Inequality Series (MESEP in Spanish) presenting its final report (DANE and DNP, 2011), after more than two-and-a-half years of work. The report consisted of a comprehensive methodology for measuring poverty, including a redesign of the monetary poverty methodology—which, as you will recall, gave way to a crisis in 2006 and 2007—and a proposal to adopt an additional index: the C-MPI.

We decided to launch the new index on August 24, 2011, at an international seminar organized by the DNP in Bogotá titled "Poverty Reduction and Promotion of Equity and Social Mobility in Colombia." Sabina Alkire and James Foster, the creators of the methodology that made the new index possible, joined us as special guests. At the event, I had the pleasant opportunity to meet them and speak with them. I expressed my enthusiasm about the new measure we were adopting and my gratitude for their advice. Like me, they were excited. It was the first time that a country had officially adopted an MPI calculated with the Alkire–Foster methodology.

In my speech, I emphasized that poverty reduction was the most important aim and a cross-cutting objective of the recently adopted National Development Plan. I said that targeted action was essential to reduce poverty, the same kind of action that made the new methodology we were introducing possible.

"Without targeted action," I stated, "it is very difficult to fight poverty. For that reason, we have also tried to innovate and create some procedures and policies to fight extreme poverty" (Santos, 2011).

By the time the seminar was held, we had set ambitious poverty reduction targets for my first four-year term, which ended in 2014. These were:

- to reduce monetary poverty from 40.3% (in 2009) to 32%;
- to reduce extreme poverty from 14.4% (in 2009) to 9.5%;
- to reduce multidimensional poverty (C-MPI) from a baseline of 34.6% (calculated for 2009) to 22.4%.

According to the DANE's reports (2015), all three targets were surpassed. By 2014:

- monetary poverty had dropped to 28.5%;[8]
- extreme poverty had dropped to 8.1%;[9]
- multidimensional poverty had dropped to 21.9%.[10]

We were doing something right with our social policy! Much of this progress had to do with properly targeting social investment, which the C-MPI and the monitoring and evaluation mechanisms that I will refer to later made possible.

Institutional Responsibilities

Colombia has an advisory planning body, which operates under the leadership of the president, in addition to involving the vice-president, all the ministers, and the head of the DNP, among other authorities. This body is the National Council for Economic and Social Policy (CONPES in Spanish). The documents it approves—known as CONPES documents—are a fundamental guide for implementing government policies and programs.[11]

The C-MPI had already been included as a strategic indicator in the National Development Plan, and it had already been officially introduced in line with the MESEP's recommendations. Now, all that remained was for it to be reflected in a CONPES document assigning specific responsibilities to the relevant government entities to calculate and implement it. The DNP took on the task of preparing this document. Finally, on May 28, 2012, CONPES Social No. 150, titled "Official Methodologies and Institutional Arrangements for Measuring Poverty in Colombia," was approved (CONPES, 2012).

Perhaps the most interesting aspect of this document is that it proposes defining an institutional arrangement to calculate both monetary and multidimensional poverty. Until then, the DNP had been responsible for designing and estimating the C-MPI, which was based, of course, on ECV statistical data provided by the DANE, the country's main statistical entity.

---

[8] According to the MESEP methodology, in effect until 2018.
[9] According to the MESEP methodology.
[10] Percentage based on the projections of the 2005 National Population and Housing Census.
[11] CONPES was created by Law 19 of 1958. It is the highest national planning authority and serves as an advisory body to the government in all aspects related to the country's economic and social development (DNP, 2022).

But this, clearly, was provisional. Once the C-MPI had been designed and adopted, institutional responsibilities needed to be defined and reassigned. CONPES made this recommendation, which was put into practice.

What was the institutional arrangement regarding the new multidimensional poverty index? In essence, it was the following.

Beginning in 2012, as the new coordinating entity, the DANE became responsible for estimating and publishing official multidimensional poverty figures, which the DNP had provisionally started to do.

In addition, two expert committees were created, one for each methodology: multidimensional and monetary. These committees are made up of specialists in estimating poverty rates, members of academia, supporters from multilateral organizations, and research center representatives, among others. They are coordinated by the DANE, with the DNP's participation, and have the mission of ensuring the transparency, comparability, and methodological stability of the measurements.

In a way, these expert committees continued the valuable work carried out by the MESEP between 2009 and 2011 to attain representative and reliable poverty indicators. From a technical point of view, these committees continue to verify and monitor that the methodologies for calculating the poverty indices are duly respected and applied.

In line with CONPES Social No. 150 recommendations, in 2012, the methodology for calculating multidimensional poverty was successfully transferred from the DNP to the DANE, which assumed full responsibility for estimating it, always with the validation of the committee of experts.

As the information that serves as the basis for calculating the C-MPI, the DANE continued to lead data collection using its periodic quality-of-life surveys.

Finally, the C-MPI's implementation, meaning its use to establish and implement social policies and programs, primarily corresponds to the Administrative Department for Social Prosperity (DPS in Spanish), ministries with social responsibilities, territorial entities, and the private sector. The DPS, an entity we established at the end of 2011, steers the social sector of the State and will be addressed in Chapter 3. The C-MPI has much to contribute, not only to the national government and public entities but also to society as a whole and the regions. Like any public policy, the C-MPI will only fully achieve its original aim when the nation as a whole values and takes ownership of it.

To summarize, between 2010 and 2012, Colombia took fundamental steps—pioneering steps in the world—to construct and adopt an objective poverty measure (in the words of Professor Amartya Sen) that would help us to reach our goal of reducing poverty more effectively:

(1) We designed the C-MPI, with technical support from OPHI.
(2) We included the C-MPI as a strategic indicator in the National Development Plan.
(3) We established, through a CONPES document, comprehensive institutional arrangements for this index's design, estimation, and implementation.

Based on these aspects, we developed a social policy that contributed to improving millions of Colombians' quality of life.

Lesson 2
Build on What Has Already Been Built

Modesty is not the most common virtue of government leaders, and I myself—I must confess—have fallen, like many others, into the temptation of praising my own achievements at the cost of minimizing those of others. This is the Adam complex, the megalomania that leads leaders to believe that everything good is of their making and begins with their mandate.

However, history teaches us that nations' greatest achievements are not the making of a single administration but require long-term efforts. The progress made during my eight-year presidential term is due not only to the hard work of my administration and civil society but also to previous administrations' work and advancements. That is why, when I was a minister three times and later when I was president, I operated under a premise that I made my mantra: we must build on what has already been built.

Aware of this, on August 24, 2011, when we introduced the new methodology for measuring poverty in Colombia, I stated, "We have created these mechanisms using common sense once again, taking what was done before and strengthening what we found" (Santos, 2011).

I have been a tireless advocate for good governance, which is characterized by effectiveness, transparency, efficiency, and accountability. Part of this philosophy is also learning about the previous administration's policies and programs, continuing what is being done well, improving what can be improved, and changing or eliminating what is not working.

This was the case with the C-MPI's adoption. I found the DNP in the process of designing this important index; I informed myself about it and learned about its advantages and characteristics. Based on this information, I pushed it forward and made the political decision to officially adopt it in Colombia. I also turned it into a public policy tool.

The same thing happened—to cite another example in the social sphere—with Familias en Acción (Families in Action), a program of cash transfers to the poorest families in the country to incentivize their children to attend school and have periodic nutrition check-ups. This program was born in the early 2000s, under President Andrés Pastrana. At the time, I was the minister of finance, a position that I used to contribute to developing and implementing it. A decade later, during my presidency, I not only continued the program but also expanded and strengthened it. I made it a State policy by converting this program into law.

Another similar situation took place with the peace process. The peace agreement reached between my administration and the Revolutionary Armed Forces of Colombia (FARC), the largest and oldest guerrilla army in the Western Hemisphere, was reached because we considered, among other things, the lessons learned in my predecessors' administrations. From Belisario Betancur (1982–1986) to Álvaro Uribe (2002–2010), all—absolutely all—tried processes or attempts to begin talks to end the armed conflict and demobilize the guerrilla groups. Despite this, some former presidents—such as Pastrana and Uribe—attacked and continue to attack the peace process that I led. By ignoring personal quarrels that were clearly of a political nature, I instead decided to build on what had already been built, making changes and corrections as necessary. In that way, we achieved a historic outcome.

In pursuing the essential purposes of a nation or a society, the best way to be effective is to continue previous work, if it was done well, picking up the baton and moving forward to advance toward the desired goals.

References

Alkire, S., and Foster, J. (2007). "Counting and multidimensional poverty measurement." Oxford Poverty and Human Development Initiative (OPHI), OPHI Working Paper 7.

Alkire, S., and Robson, M. (2018). "On data availability for assessing monetary and multidimensional poverty." OPHI Research in Progress Series 52a, September. https://ophi.org.uk/on-data-availability-for-assessing-monetary-and-multidimensional-poverty.

Angulo, R. (2011). "La medición de la pobreza en Colombia: Respuestas para el debate." Razón Pública, October 9. https://razonpublica.com/la-medicion-de-la-pobreza-en-colombia-respuestas-para-el-debate.

Angulo, R. (2016). "From multidimensional poverty measurement to multisector public policy for poverty reduction: Lessons from the Colombian case." University of Oxford, OPHI Working Paper 102, February. https://www.ophi.org.uk/wp-content/uploads/OPHIWP102_1.pdf.

Angulo, R., and Zavaleta, D. (2018). "Colombia: Building scenarios for setting MPI goals: From multidimensional measurement to multisector public policy." *Dimensions*, 5, 17–20. https://mppn.org/wp-content/uploads/2018/11/Dimensions-Nov-2018._EN_webversion.pdf.

Angulo, R., Díaz, Y., and Pardo, R. (2011). "Índice de Pobreza Multidimensional para Colombia (IPM-Colombia) 1997–2010." Archivos de Economía 382, November 8. https://colaboracion.dnp.gov.co/cdt/estudios%20econmicos/382.pdf.

Angulo, R., Díaz, Y., and Pardo, R. (2016). "The Colombian Multidimensional Poverty Index: Measuring poverty in a public policy context." *Social Indicators Research*, 127, 1–38. https://doi.org/10.1007/s11205-015-0964-z.

Congreso de la República de Colombia. (2011). "Ley 1450—Plan Nacional de Desarrollo, 2010–2014." *Diario Oficial*, 48, 102.

CONPES (National Council for Economic and Social Policy), & DNP (National Planning Department). (2012). "Metodologías oficiales y arreglos institucionales para la medición de la pobreza en Colombia." Documento CONPES Social 150, May 28. https://colaboracion.dnp.gov.co/CDT/Conpes/Social/150.pdf.

Costa Rica Gobierno del Bicentenario, Ministerio de Planificación Nacional y Política Económica, and Ministerio de Hacienda Costa Rica. (2019). "Lineamientos técnicos y metodológicos para la planificación, programación presupuestaria, seguimiento y la evaluación estratégica en el Sector Público en Costa Rica 2020." MIDEPLAN. https://documentos.mideplan.go.cr/share/s/OioRReBlRTKqaeSm7OexyQ.

DANE (National Administrative Department of Statistics). (2015). "Pobreza Monetaria y Multidimensional en Colombia 2014. Boletín Técnico." March 24. https://www.dane.gov.co/files/investigaciones/condiciones_vida/pobreza/bol_pobreza_14_.pdf

DANE (2019a). "COLOMBIA—Encuesta Nacional de Calidad de Vida—ECV 2018." April 30. http://microdatos.dane.gov.co/index.php/catalog/607/study-description.

DANE. (2019b). "Boletín técnico pobreza monetaria departamental." July 12. https://www.dane.gov.co/files/investigaciones/condiciones_vida/pobreza/2018/bt_pobreza_monetaria_18_departamentos.pdf.

DANE, and DNP. (2011). "Pobreza monetaria en Colombia: Nueva metodología y cifras 2002–2010." Misión para el Empalme de las Series de Empleo, Pobreza y Desigualdad (MESEP). https://www.dane.gov.co/files/noticias/Pobreza_nuevametodologia.pdf.

DNP. (2010). "National Development Plan 2010–2014, 'Prosperity for all.' Executive summary." https://colaboracion.dnp.gov.co/CDT/PND/Resumen_Ejecutivo_Definitivo_PND%20en%20ingl%C3%A9s06-07-2011.pdf.

DNP. (2017). "Pobreza monetaria y multidimensional departamental: Necesidad de políticas públicas diferenciadas." Panorámica Regional (3rd edn), April. https://colaboracion.dnp.gov.co/CDT/Desarrollo%20Territorial/Portal%20Territorial/KitSeguimiento/Pobreza/Publicaci%C3%B3n%20Ipm%20deptal.pdf.

DNP. (2022). "El Consejo Nacional de Política Económica y Social, CONPES." https://www.dnp.gov.co/CONPES/Paginas/conpes.aspx.

Evans, M., Nogales, R., and Robson, M. (2020). "Monetary and multidimensional poverty: Correlations, mismatches, and joint distributions." University of Oxford, OPHI Working Paper 133.

Gaddis, I., and Klasen, S. (2012). "Mapping MPI and monetary poverty: The case of Uganda" [PowerPoint slides]. November 21–22. https://www.ophi.org.uk/wp-content/uploads/Stephan-Klasen-Mapping-MPI-and-Monetary-Poverty-The-Case-of-Uganda.pdf.

Gajardo, F. (2013). "Pobreza en Chile: ¿Se está midiendo a quienes viven bajo el fenómeno de pobreza?" [thesis]. Universidad de Chile. https://repositorio.uchile.cl/bitstream/handle/2250/112198/Tesis%20Felipe%20Gajardo%20Le%C3%B3n.pdf.

Salecker, L., Ahmadov, A. K., and Karimli, L. (2020). "Contrasting monetary and multidimensional poverty measures in a low-income Sub-Saharan African country." Social Indicators Research, 151, 547–574. https://doi.org/10.1007/s11205-020-02382-z.

Santos, J. M. (2011). "Palabras del presidente Juan Manuel Santos en el lanzamiento del Índice de Pobreza Multidimensional, la nueva Línea de Pobreza y la Misión de Movilidad Social" [speech transcript]. Presidencia República de Colombia, August 24. http://wsp.presidencia.gov.co/Prensa/2011/Agosto/Paginas/20110824_03.aspx.

Sen, A. (1981). Poverty and famines: An essay on entitlement and deprivation. Clarendon Press.

Sen, A. (1997). On economic inequality. Clarendon Press.

Sen, A. (1999). Development as freedom. Oxford University Press.

Suppa, N. (2016). "Comparing monetary and multidimensional poverty in Germany." University of Oxford, OPHI Working Paper 103. https://www.ophi.org.uk/wp-content/uploads/OPHIWP103_1.pdf.

Tran, V. Q., Alkire, S., and Klasen, S. (2015). "Static and dynamic disparities between monetary and multidimensional poverty measurement: Evidence from Vietnam." University of Oxford, OPHI Working Paper 97, August. https://ophi.org.uk/static-and-dynamic-disparities-between-monetary-and-multidimensional-poverty-measurement-evidence-from-vietnam.

3
Institutional Design to Combat Poverty

A Commitment to Victims

Political capital is for spending. That's what I had in mind when I began my term as president of Colombia on August 7, 2010, and it's why I swiftly and resolutely took on the most difficult tasks in the first months of my administration. Specifically, I made progress on two fronts: first, with absolute discretion, contacting the Revolutionary Armed Forces of Colombia (FARC) guerrilla army to lay the foundations for a peace process, and second, establishing the necessary legal instruments and institutional structure to fight poverty and promote equity.

One group in particular appeared to be at the intersection of these two objectives: the victims. The internal armed conflict had destroyed homes, displaced millions of people throughout the country, and spread pain and destitution in rural and border areas. War and poverty go hand in hand. Therefore, one of my administration's initial commitments was to issue a law on victims and land restitution that would seek to compensate the people who had been most affected by the armed conflict.

Between 2007 and 2009, the Liberal Party in Congress had promoted a bill for a victims' law to this end. However, under the pretext that it had a high budget, President Uribe's administration did not support it, and the bill failed.

Determined to rectify this situation, on September 27, 2010, I introduced a bill in Congress for a Victims' Law, which to date had been small-mindedly denied to the Colombians who deserved it the most. I didn't introduce it in just any way. I gave a speech in the Plaza de Armas outside the Palacio de Nariño, the presidential house, explaining the bill's importance, and I walked to the National Capitol with the leaders of the political parties that made up the government coalition, where I personally submitted the bill to begin its legislative process.

The Battle Against Poverty. Juan Manuel Santos, Oxford University Press. © Juan Manuel Santos (2023).
DOI: 10.1093/oso/9780192885234.003.0004

It was an essential issue for Colombia's future and to begin setting the stage for possible national reconciliation. Therefore, in my speech, I spoke these words, which echoed in Congress and in the country:

> If we successfully pass this law and abide by it, in the interest of all our victims—if we do only this!—it will have been worth it for me to be president, and for you, congressional representatives, to have been elected to your seats.

(Santos, 2010)

Later, during the debate on this bill for a victims' law, the inconsistency between seeking to compensate armed conflict victims and maintaining the previous administration's position—denying the conflict's existence and referring to it only as a terrorist threat—was made clear. Aware of this, I stated the obvious: in Colombia, we were experiencing an internal armed conflict, and the aim of the law we were promoting was, precisely, to extend a hand to the hundreds of thousands of Colombians affected by this conflict. Recognizing the existence of an internal armed conflict was also a necessary condition for invoking the Rome Statute and implementing transitional justice in a potential peace process.

Decisions such as these—to promote the Victims' Law and to recognize the existence of the internal armed conflict—led to my presidential predecessor's distancing and criticism, but they laid the foundations for my primary goals: to move toward peace and toward significant poverty reduction.

Finally, Congress passed a law that sought not only to compensate victims of the conflict but also to support displaced small-scale farmers to return to the plots that had been stolen from them. It was Law 1448 of 2011, known as the Victims and Land Restitution Law, a historic initiative applauded and supported by the international community. As evidence of this support, United Nations Secretary General Ban Ki-moon came to Bogotá to witness the law's enactment ceremony, which we held on June 10, 2011, in the same Plaza de Armas where we had announced the bill's introduction just over eight months before.

On that day, before an audience that excitedly supported this dream becoming a reality, I stated, "If we have had victims, if people continue to be victimized, we will put ourselves and stand on the right side: next to them, on their side, embracing and understanding their suffering" (Santos, 2011a).

Background on State Social Policy Coordination

Among other measures, the Victims' Law established a Unit for Comprehensive Care and Reparation for Victims, which formed part of a National System for Comprehensive Care and Reparation for Victims (SNARIV in Spanish). It was no small task: Colombia has recognized more than 9 million victims of the internal armed conflict to date. The law also established a National Center for Historical Memory, entrusted with compiling, analyzing, and storing documents and testimonies about the conflict.

But this law wasn't only about the victims. It went further than that. We were aware that SNARIV couldn't be understood separately from the goal of reducing poverty and inequality in the country since the victims were, in many cases, the most significant sign of this poverty and inequality. Efforts to support victims and displaced persons needed to be linked to national efforts to improve Colombians' living conditions, protect vulnerable children, and substantially reduce poverty, particularly extreme poverty.

We must not forget that in August 2011, two months after the Victims and Land Restitution Law's enactment, we launched the new Colombian Multidimensional Poverty Index (C-MPI), always with the aim of adding and refining more instruments to improve social equity. Various government efforts were heading in the same direction but now required a strong institutional structure for coordinating actions carried out by the different entities.

With this in mind, the Victims' Law included an article (Article 170) titled "Transition of the Institutional Structure." It stipulated the following:

> During the year following this law's entry into force, the national government must make the required institutional reforms in the entities and bodies that currently perform duties related to the matters covered by this law, in order to avoid the duplication of duties and ensure continuity of service without affecting care for the victims at any time. The Presidential Agency for Social Action and International Cooperation will be transformed into an administrative department that will be responsible for setting policies, overall plans, programs, and projects for assistance, care, and reparation for victims of the violations referred to in Article 3 of this law, social inclusion, care for vulnerable groups, and social and economic reintegration.
>
> (Ley 1448 de 2011)

What did this mean in practice? It meant the establishment of a robust institutional structure, headed by an administrative department—which, in Colombia, is a public entity in the same category as a ministry and with the same importance—to establish policies, plans, programs, and projects. These would address not only assistance, care, and reparation for victims of the armed conflict but also social inclusion, care for vulnerable groups, and social and economic reintegration.

Until then, a presidential agency with limited decision-making power and no autonomy had been in charge of central coordination of the State's social policies. In 1994, President Ernesto Samper had created the Social Solidarity Network, based on the model of Mexico's National Solidarity Program (PRONASOL in Spanish), which President Carlos Salinas de Gortari's administration began to promote in 1989. The Social Solidarity Network achieved important results, but it also faced problems in implementing its programs due to "budget gaps, excessive bureaucratization, lack of interinstitutional coordination, and political influence in resource distribution" (Jaramillo, 2012).

In July 2005, during President Álvaro Uribe's first term, the Social Solidarity Network merged with the Colombian Agency for International Cooperation (bearing in mind that the bulk of this cooperation is allocated for social purposes), giving rise to a new entity still within the arena of the Office of the President: the Presidential Agency for Social Action and International Cooperation, known as Acción Social. For budget purposes, this entity was assigned the Investment Fund for Peace (FIP in Spanish). This fund had been created in 1998 to finance peace efforts made by the Andrés Pastrana administration.

That was the situation when I assumed the presidency in August 2010. Both the Social Solidarity Network, during its time, and, subsequently, Acción Social had been steps in the right direction; they had produced positive results, albeit insufficient, in the fight against poverty. To advance more effective and stronger policies, we proposed a solution to transition from having a presidential agency—without real teeth for acting and coordinating—to establishing a sector within the State that, unbelievably, did not yet exist.

There were many sectors: defense and security, education, infrastructure, health, and others but no sector exclusively dedicated to coordinating efforts to support the most vulnerable populations and reduce poverty.

Thus, exercising the extraordinary powers that Congress had given me to modify the public administration structure and complying with Article 170 of the Victims' Law, I issued Decree 4155 on November 3, 2011. Under this decree, Acción Social transitioned from being a presidential agency to being an administrative department in charge of a new State sector: the Administrative Department for Social Prosperity (DPS in Spanish), the main and governing body of an administrative sector for social inclusion and reconciliation.

High-Level Advice

In July 2010, one month before taking office as president of Colombia, I traveled to London. There, as president-elect, I met with Prime Minister David Cameron and my good friend Tony Blair, former prime minister.

In 1999, Blair and I had published a book in favor of the Third Way, the economic and political doctrine inspired by Anthony Giddens, former head of my alma mater, the London School of Economics. This doctrine advocates for a pragmatic approach to the State–market dilemma. The phrase "the market to the extent possible, the State to the extent necessary" summarizes this middle-of-the-road approach on which Blair and I agreed. A few years later, on July 1, 2014, I brought together five former heads of state in Cartagena: Bill Clinton from the United States, Felipe González from Spain, Fernando Henrique Cardoso from Brazil, Ricardo Lagos from Chile, and of course, Tony Blair from the United Kingdom. In practice, they had been the most important exponents of the Third Way, and under their leadership, coincidentally or not, their countries had obtained the best economic and social results.

I went to visit Blair in his office, accompanied by our then ambassador in London, my brother-in-law Mauricio Rodríguez (whom I had not appointed). We had a friendly and relaxed meeting.

I remember that Blair said to me:

> Juan Manuel, now that you've won the elections and are preparing to govern your country, I have good news and bad news. The good news is that you've won, and you'll be able to implement your government agenda to improve Colombians' lives. The bad news is that the honeymoon doesn't last longer than six months, a year at the most. So, I advise you to introduce and drive forward any important reforms you are going to try as quickly as possible.

They were wise words, spoken in good faith by a man who had been leading the United Kingdom's future for more than ten years, and they stuck with me. As soon as I took office, I began my work to reform and modernize the State, aiming to set into motion what we had called in the campaign "engines of prosperity." I asked Blair to help me. At the beginning of his second term, in 2001, he had led an interesting innovation: the establishment of a performance-monitoring unit within his government, in the very office of the prime minister and under his direct supervision. It was called the

Prime Minister's Delivery Unit. This unit's aim was to guarantee the implementation and fulfillment of the government's priority policies. Admittedly, it was successful, helping many ambitious policies proposed by Blair come to fruition. I wanted to do something similar in Colombia.

Blair sent several of his closest advisors to Bogotá, who met with me and my administration's senior officials. They proposed concrete ideas to have a more agile and effective State structure. Blair himself came to Colombia in April 2011. I convened my ministers to listen to and dialogue with him, and we had a long and interesting exchange of ideas, not only about government policies but also about international politics. At the end of our meeting, I gave him a well-deserved award for his continued support to Colombia: the Order of Boyacá, which is the highest decoration awarded in my country. One of the advisors who came with him, Jonathan Powell, his former chief of staff and a negotiator in Northern Ireland, became one of my top advisors in the peace process we were advancing in Colombia. This process ended a war with the most powerful and oldest guerrilla army in the Western Hemisphere that had lasted for over 50 years.

Many of the ideas proposed by Blair and his advisors were ultimately reflected in our 2011 reform of the State reform, which affected key sectors for economic development, social inclusion, and job creation. Among other initiatives, we created the National Infrastructure Agency, the National Mining Agency, the National Agency for Legal Defense of the State, the National Intelligence Directorate, the National Public Procurement Agency (Colombia Compra Eficiente, a system we copied from Chile), and the National Unit for Disaster Risk Management. We reversed an austerity-oriented measure by the previous administration that had merged ministries. This measure ultimately proved to be counterproductive since a ministry with multiple portfolios is less effective. For the same reason, we recreated the following as separate entities: the Ministry of the Interior; the Ministry of Justice and Law; the Ministry of Labor; the Ministry of Health and Social Protection; the Ministry of Environment and Sustainable Development; and the Ministry of Housing, City, and Territory. And an essential piece, directed at my administration's priority of advancing equity: we created the social inclusion and reconciliation sector.

Today, I thank Tony Blair for his timely advice because it made me wake up to the reality that major reforms must be proposed and implemented at the beginning of a mandate. Of course, I also thank his advisors, who helped us find an agile and novel institutional design that would produce true and measurable results.

A New State Sector: Social Inclusion and Reconciliation

On November 9, 2011, at a packed ceremony in the El Campín arena in Bogotá, I introduced the social inclusion and reconciliation sector in Colombia, destined to improve the lives of millions of Colombians.

I said that war and poverty go hand in hand. It was time to demonstrate that, when working smoothly, another alliance—peace and social inclusion—could counteract the disasters of war and poverty.

The senior presidential advisor for good governance, María Lorena Gutiérrez, and the director of Acción Social at the time were responsible for organizing and designing the new sector, with support from the National Planning Department and the Administrative Department of Public Service. The goal of establishing this sector was to create a cross-cutting vision of the fight against poverty, coordinated by the DPS, to guarantee that each ministry and administrative department made concrete contributions in its area to this countrywide work.

An excerpt from the words I spoke on that November day, in front of thousands of beneficiaries of government social programs, summarizes the spirit of our reform:

Poverty is our main challenge, our nation's main challenge, and we have to face it with all the tools of the State and society.

Reducing poverty must be a commitment not only of the government, but also of all Colombians: businesspeople, trade unions, social and community organizations, each and every one of us.

Today, for that reason, we have gathered to tell Colombia and the world that poverty reduction is our number one goal and that we finally have an institutional structure in the State that reflects the importance of this issue.

Until now, efforts to fight poverty were, in a way, scattered across the State.

We had Acción Social—a very important entity that made an enormous and hardworking effort to support programs such as Red Unidos (United Network), Familias en Acción (Families in Action), Familias Guardabosques (Forest-Guard Families), and assistance for displaced persons and their return to their lands, among many others.

We had the Office of the Presidential Advisor for Social Prosperity, which coordinated poverty reduction—especially extreme poverty reduction—from the top level of the government.

We had, of course, the Colombian Family Welfare Institute, with its important programs for children, mothers, and families in general.

We had social consolidation programs in the areas most affected by violence, once the armed forces took back these areas.

And now, we have the enormous challenge of implementing the Victims' Law, which will seek to provide reparations to hundreds of thousands of people affected by the violence in our country.

(Santos, 2011b)

Based on these premises (i.e. the list of entities that worked separately to combat poverty and provide aid to the country's most vulnerable populations), I went on to announce the establishment of a new sector that brought them all together:

All this made us reflect that, if we want the fight against poverty to be successful, it requires coordination at the highest level.

The fight against poverty must be coordinated by a ministerial-level entity and involve other affiliated entities that support this work, which—I repeat—is the State's primary task.

Therefore, with the powers that Congress gave us to reform the State, we have established not just one entity but an entire sector: the social inclusion and reconciliation sector.

Today, we have a sector to fight poverty, and it is led by a new entity: the Department for Social Prosperity.

And when I say we have a sector, I mean that we have defined a group of entities, with a coordinating body, that will design and work exclusively on reducing poverty and setting the scene for reconciliation and peace in the areas where violence ruled.

To establish this sector, we drew upon many successful experiences across the world, such as in Brazil, Mexico, and Chile, and we adapted them to our country's unique features.

How will the social inclusion and reconciliation sector operate?

Essentially, there will be a lead entity: the Administrative Department for Social Prosperity. Other entities affiliated with this department will focus on special issues, such as care and reparations for victims, protection of children and families, work to lift hundreds of thousands of families out of extreme poverty, and the consolidation of a comprehensive State presence in areas taken back.

The Administrative Department for Social Prosperity—which, I repeat, is as important as a ministry—will coordinate its affiliated entities' work and directly lead strategies such as Families in Action.

(Santos, 2011b)

The Administrative Department for Social Prosperity

As already mentioned, the Administrative Department for Social Prosperity (DPS in Spanish) was established to lead this new sector, building on the experience of the Presidential Agency for Social Action and International Cooperation, known as Acción Social, up until then.

Its establishment, as well as the new sector's establishment, was part of implementing the 2010–2014 National Development Plan, "Prosperity for All," which we introduced in Congress and which had become law. The plan set out a navigation map for my first term as president, with the overall objective of coordinating economic development ("Prosperity") with social inclusion ("for All"). To this end, four challenges were identified:

> (a) increase the efficiency of social spending so that resources translate into better results in terms of coverage and quality; (b) improve the targeting of social spending so that it primarily benefits the most poor and vulnerable; (c) consolidate a social protection system that effectively contributes to strengthening human capital and household income and to reducing households' vulnerability; and (d) achieve the social inclusion of different ethnic groups, as well as gender equality.
>
> (DNP, 2010, p. 322)

As the sector's head institution, the new DPS became responsible for establishing policies, plans, programs, and projects for social inclusion and reconciliation. This encompassed work to overcome poverty and extreme poverty; care for vulnerable groups; comprehensive care for early childhood, childhood, and adolescence; territorial development; and care and reparation for victims of the armed conflict. Of course, to carry out such important tasks, the DPS included some affiliated units and institutions that I will refer to later.

Nevertheless, some high-social-impact programs were not delegated to the affiliated entities but directly led by the DPS. This is the case of Families in Action, a cash-transfer program for the country's poorest families. The transfers are conditioned upon parents sending their children to school and taking them to periodic growth-and-development check-ups as well as vaccination programs. This program, which began to be implemented in 2000, back when I was the minister of finance, has become an essential partner in the fight against poverty, given that it not only helps poor families economically but also guarantees and encourages children's school attendance and health check-ups. By the time we created the DPS, the program was benefiting more than 2.5 million families in the country.

The DPS also took charge of other programs, such as Mujeres Ahorradoras (Women Savers) and Empleo de Emergencia (Emergency Employment), which aimed to create nearly 100,000 jobs for the poorest people. Similarly, it took over the Red de Seguridad Alimentaria (Food Security Network) program to improve nutrition among the poorest families.

Other Entities, New Responsibilities

Which entities were affiliated with the new DPS, now forming part of a large social inclusion and reconciliation sector?

Initially, there were five: the Colombian Family Welfare Institute, the National Agency for Overcoming Extreme Poverty, the Unit for Comprehensive Care and Reparation for Victims, the National Center for Historical Memory, and the Unit for Territorial Consolidation.

The **Colombian Family Welfare Institute** (ICBF in Spanish) is a long-standing institution in Colombia, created by the Carlos Lleras administration in 1968 to look after the care and protection of vulnerable children. In carrying out its mission, the institute benefits millions of children by delivering breakfasts and lunches to child-care centers and public educational institutions; by taking care of children who do not have a responsible adult to care for them, using special homes or foster families; by maintaining the Madres Comunitarias (Community Mothers) program, in which properly trained women take care of their neighbors' children so these neighbors can work; and, very importantly, by implementing a comprehensive early childhood care program.

In my administration, we placed special emphasis on caring for children in their first stage of life, meaning from their fetal development until five years of age, since evidence has shown that this is the time when they develop skills to thrive and be happy. My wife, María Clemencia, led an initiative called "De Cero a Siempre" ("From Zero to Forever") to this end; as a result, 274 child development centers were established and equipped throughout the country, and the goal of providing comprehensive early childhood care to nearly 1.5 million children was met. American professor James Heckman, a Nobel laureate in economics, joined us in Bogotá during this initiative's launch in February 2011. In his studies, he has posited the importance of society's investment in early childhood care. According to Professor Heckman, timely action fosters school attendance, reduces crime rates, promotes workforce productivity, and lowers adolescent pregnancy rates. As a good economist, he argues that this is the most profitable social investment for any nation or people.

Undoubtedly, the ICBF is one of the crown jewels in implementing Colombian social policy due to its constant work in favor of children.

The second entity that made up the social sector coordinated by the DPS was the **National Agency for Overcoming Extreme Poverty** (ANSPE in Spanish). We established this agency based on what, until then, had been an advisory office: the Office of the Presidential Advisor for Social Prosperity.

This new agency aimed to implement a strategy for overcoming extreme poverty, which the advisory office had designed, with a tangible target: to lift at least 350,000 families—more than 1.5 million Colombians—out of extreme poverty. In 14 months, my administration had already lowered the unemployment rate to a single-digit figure. Our commitment was to also lower the extreme poverty rate to a single-digit figure, and we succeeded. The proportion of Colombians in extreme poverty had been 14.4% in 2009 and 12.3% in 2010. In 2013, we lowered it to 9.1%, and in 2018, the last year of my mandate, it was at 7.2%.[1]

With the ANSPE's establishment, there was now an entity responsible for the policy to overcome extreme poverty, focused on lifting hundreds of thousands of families out of this situation. The main tool to accomplish this objective was the Red Unidos (United Network), based on the Red Juntos (Together Network) that had been created in 2007. Red Unidos is a strategy for coordination among State entities to support families living in extreme poverty and provide them with all available social benefits until they are able to rise out of poverty. It operates through a large group of caseworkers—more than 10,000, who I called my "social army"—that visit each one of these families across the country, inform them about support programs, help them sign up, and conduct personalized follow-up to assess their situation and progress. At the time of the ANSPE's establishment, Red Unidos brought together more than one million families across the country. These families, with the proper support, were in the process of overcoming extreme poverty and reaching sustainability.

The third entity in the sector was the recently established **Unit for Comprehensive Care and Reparation for Victims**.

The new Victims' Law began to be implemented on January 1, 2012, with the monumental task of providing reparation and improving the situation of

---

[1] According to the MESEP methodology, which is the only one that enables comparisons with figures from years before 2012.

millions of Colombians who had lost a lot or everything in the past decades of the armed conflict. The Victims' Unit had the mission of implementing the mechanisms laid out in the law for providing economic, social, and moral compensation to Colombians affected by the violence; its mission had to be completed in ten years or, in other words, by December 31, 2021, although this period was extended in 2021 for an additional ten years.

Led by its director, Paula Gaviria, a lawyer who is also the granddaughter of former President Belisario Betancur, the first to attempt peace negotiations with the FARC guerrillas, the unit set out to identify and register more than 9 million victims of the conflict and begin providing reparations to them. In August 2018, at the end of my mandate, we had delivered humanitarian assistance and aid to 4 million victims and provided economic compensation to 900,000.

A fourth entity affiliated with the DPS, also related to the conflict, was the **National Center for Historical Memory**. If Colombia were to compensate its victims, part of that compensation had to involve reconstructing our memory as Colombians, remembering and elucidating what happened—and thus ensuring that it never happens again: the right to non-repetition. As this center's head, I appointed the sociologist and historian Gonzalo Sánchez, who had a long career in researching and disseminating the terrible events that took place during the Colombian conflict. Unfortunately, my successor, President Iván Duque, appointed a person to succeed Sánchez who demonstrated a clear ideological bias and wanted to push aside the good work that had been performed for this fundamentally restorative task.

The fifth entity affiliated with the DPS, within the new social sector, was the **Unit for Territorial Consolidation**. This unit aimed to coordinate efforts to consolidate a State presence in the areas taken back from violent groups.

When I was the minister of defense between 2006 and 2009, I promoted a territorial consolidation policy in regions affected by the war, such as the Macarena region, a mountain range where Andean, Amazonian, and Orinoquía ecosystems come together; the Montes de María region in the Caribbean; and southern Tolima in the country's central region. The aim was to bring State presence, including security as well as social and justice services, to areas we were taking back from the control of guerrillas and other armed groups. There, the armed forces worked hand in hand with all the ministries and State agencies, as well as civil society, to build livelihood projects and provide basic utility services to the population.

The establishment of the Unit for Territorial Consolidation arose from the need to have a coordinating entity that would guarantee the sustainability of these processes. This unit also coordinated the Forest-Guard Families program, which complemented initiatives for the manual eradication of illicit crops. As director of this unit, I appointed the economist and field expert Álvaro Balcázar, who had previously been in charge of the consolidation plan we created at the Ministry of Defense.

In this way, with these five entities and the overall coordination of the DPS, we gave the go-ahead to the social inclusion and reconciliation sector in November 2011. This represented an important reform of Colombia's institutional structure, based on its results, some say the most important, which facilitated achieving the ambitious goals to reduce poverty and inequality that we had set for ourselves.

Of the six entities making up the social sector—the DPS and its five affiliated entities—four remain today, more than a decade after this reform. The DPS continues to be the leading social policy entity in the country, the ICBF continues its admirable work to protect vulnerable children, the Victims' Unit maintains its mission to care for and provide reparations to the victims of the armed conflict, with a time frame that, as I said, was extended until December 2031, and the National Center for Historical Memory persists in its work to compile, analyze, and disseminate what happened during the decades of internal war. As for the ANSPE and the Unit for Territorial Consolidation, they merged with the DPS in early 2016 for reasons of efficiency. Consequently, the DPS took over the responsibility of managing the program to overcome extreme poverty through Red Unidos—the most emblematic program in the fight to reduce extreme poverty.

Without a doubt, the new sector was instrumental in making progress toward overcoming poverty, but it cannot accomplish this work alone. The State, as a whole, must contribute to this priority objective. This requires each sector—for example, health, housing, education, culture—to make contributions from its field of action. To coordinate and monitor this cross-cutting work, the Poverty Roundtable and the dashboards I will refer to in Chapter 4 would be fundamental.

"The Executioner of Poverty"

To continue my account of what the establishment of the social sector in Colombia meant, I quote my final words from a speech on November 9, 2011, in which I announced the new sector.

Just five days beforehand, special commands of our armed forces had attacked the hideout of Alfonso Cano, the FARC's commander-in-chief, and killed him. Therefore, after reiterating the promise I made on my inauguration day that I would not fail the poor of Colombia, I shared a final reflection:

> Now that Cano has fallen, some media have said that I will go down in history as the "FARC executioner."
>
> Today, I want to say that it's very important to strike back at terrorism, and we are committed to doing so.
>
> But that's not how I want to go down in history.
>
> I'd like you to remember our administration as the one that lowered the unemployment rate to a single digit and created more than two million decent jobs for Colombians.
>
> I'd like you to remember our administration as the one that lowered the extreme poverty rate to a single digit and lifted hundreds of thousands of families out of this situation.
>
> I'd like you to remember our administration as the one that finally began providing reparations to victims and land restitution for those who were dispossessed.
>
> I'd like you to remember our administration as the one that brought State services to the most forgotten areas of the country.
>
> So, if I'm going to be an executioner, I prefer to be the "executioner of poverty."
>
> If so, I assure you, I'll be the happiest man on Earth.
>
> With the new social inclusion and reconciliation sector, with the new Department for Social Prosperity and its affiliated entities, a new era begins for Colombia.
>
> (Santos, 2011b)

Ability to Govern: Key Agreements to Achieve Goals

I began this chapter by stating that political capital is for spending, and I devoted myself to that in the first months of my mandate. That start-up time is the best time to propose and make the most impactful reforms since it is when you have the most popularity and a majority in Congress—in other words, the ability to govern—that, later on, due to political exhaustion, begin losing strength. But the "ability to govern" must not be taken for granted. It must be built, and that's what I did.

When I took office as president on August 7, 2010, I remembered an excellent biography I had recently read: *Team of Rivals: The Political Genius of Abraham Lincoln* by the historian Doris Kearns Goodwin. Steven Spielberg based his acclaimed film *Lincoln* on this book. Goodwin notes that Lincoln, after winning the Republican presidential nomination in 1860 and then becoming president, appointed his rivals for the nomination to high positions of his cabinet. As a result, he maintained the unity of his party and gained the ability to govern (enough votes in Congress) and to promote reforms as significant as the abolition of slavery.

Inspired by that example, when I took office, backed by the party I had founded a few years earlier, the Social Party of National Unity (known as the "U Party"), I understood that, if I really wanted to transform the country, I had to reach early agreements that would ensure the majority I needed in Congress. Therefore, I invited former contenders I had faced in the first round of presidential elections, such as Rafael Pardo, who had been a candidate for the Liberal Party, and Germán Vargas, who had participated on behalf of the Radical Change Party, to be part of my administration. I also called on the Conservative Party to form part of the governing coalition, and I appointed prominent members of this party to my cabinet. My call was to build a government of national unity, which would join forces and efforts to face the nation's greatest challenges.

Thanks to this, we consolidated a large and solid majority in Congress. In the first legislature I worked with during my administration, this majority made it possible to pass reforms that would have seemed unthinkable just a few years before. These reforms were aimed at promoting the three pillars of our National Development Plan: more security, more jobs, and less poverty. Among these many early reforms, I highlight the following:

- a law that granted the president extraordinary powers to reform the State, which we used to create the social inclusion and reconciliation sector, among other objectives;
- a constitutional reform on fiscal sustainability (similar to one in Germany), which gave the executive branch the possibility of rejecting decisions by Congress or the judiciary that seriously affected public finances;
- the Victims and Land Restitution Law;
- a reform of royalties, which allowed resources resulting from oil exploitation and mining to be more equitably distributed among the country's regions.

Through decrees and other administrative measures, we also made progress in social achievements for the most vulnerable populations in the first 15 months of government. I will mention some.

- We unified the health insurance scheme for Colombians over 60 years of age so that those who were in the subsidized scheme—the poorest users, who are exempt from paying into social security—were entitled to the same benefits as people in the contributory scheme. In later years, we succeeded in covering the entire population, not just older adults, under this unified scheme, thus ending the hateful distinction between first- and second-class patients. "Everyone in the first-class cabin," is what I said and did.

- We began building nearly 260,000 homes throughout the country, most of them low-income or social housing, meaning intended for the poorest families, with subsidized prices.
- We guaranteed, as of January 1, 2012, completely free public education— from grade zero[2] to grade 11, which is the last year of secondary education.

Additionally, as seen in Chapter 2, we officially adopted a new instrument for measuring poverty, the C-MPI, in August 2011, and we included it as a strategic indicator in the 2010–2014 National Development Plan.

When we launched the new social inclusion and reconciliation sector in early November 2011, it was not an isolated effort but an additional effort within a set of complementary initiatives aimed at the same purpose. Following Tony Blair's advice, we took advantage of the first year in office and the ability to govern that exists in that period to lay the legal and institutional foundations that would enable substantially reducing poverty and improving the living conditions of Colombians, especially low-income Colombians.

Lesson 3
The State Must Put Its Full Weight behind Priority Goals

Every government, if it is to be effective, must set clear priorities and focus its work accordingly. In our case, in my first term (2010–2014), these were summed up in three priorities that corresponded to Colombians' overall cry: achieve greater security, create more jobs, and reduce poverty.

Once priorities are established, it is necessary to seek synergy between various State bodies and within the administration itself to advance toward making them a reality. In our case, we reached a successful level of coordination and obtained the ability to govern through strategic political alliances that enabled advancing progressive and innovative legislation on issues such

[2] In Colombia, "grade zero" refers to a transitional year of schooling for five-year-old children before they begin primary school (first grade). Attendance is compulsory. Before grade zero, children may attend preschool or kindergarten, which is non-compulsory.

as reparations for victims and the reform of State institutions. But we also moved in the direction of synchronizing various government entities in pursuit of the stated objectives.

It is not enough for each entity to fulfill its work or the mission set out in its founding statutes. There must be sectors and coordinating bodies that ensure efforts are not isolated—and, as a result, sometimes contradictory and exclusive—but all go in the same direction, as efforts contributing to the work of transforming society toward greater standards of equity and justice.

For that reason, we created the social inclusion and reconciliation sector in 2011, coordinated by a ministerial-level entity: the Administrative Department for Social Prosperity, under the supervision of the president himself. We did this to ensure that the State put its full weight behind working to achieve priority goals and that such work was effective and efficient.

This new institutional structure was established for a specific aim: to coordinate, at the highest level, the fight against poverty and to work for the country's most vulnerable populations.

References

Decreto 1084 de 2015. (2015). "Sector de inclusión social y reconciliación." Departamento Administrativo de la Función Pública, May 26. https://www.funcionpublica.gov.co/eva/gestornormativo/norma.php?i=77715.

Departamento Administrativo de la Función Pública. (2018). "Análisis sector inclusión social y reconciliación" [PowerPoint slides]. November 2. https://www.funcionpublica.gov.co/documents/34645357/34704716/analisis-sector-inclusion-social-reconciliacion.pdf/f48a2ff1-fb10-473d-ac0a-58309546d30e?version=1.0&t=1543336905120.

Departamento Administrativo de la Función Pública. (n.d.). "Sector de inclusión social y reconciliación. Manual de estructura del Estado." https://www.funcionpublica.gov.co/eva/gestornormativo/manual-estado/pdf/23_Sector_Inclusion_Social_y_Reconciliacion.pdf#page=1.

DNP (National Planning Department). (2010). "Plan Nacional de Desarrollo 2010–2014. 'Prosperidad para todos,' Tomo I." https://colaboracion.dnp.gov.co/CDT/PND/PND2010-2014%20Tomo%20I%20CD.pdf.

Jaramillo Londoño, C. (2012). "Red de Solidaridad Social en Colombia." *Revista Universidad EAFIT*, 33(105), 127–141.

Ley 1448 de 2011. (2011). "Por la cual se dictan medidas de atención, asistencia y reparación integral a las víctimas del conflicto armado interno y se dictan otras disposiciones." Presidencia de la República de Colombia, June 10.

http://wp.presidencia.gov.co/sitios/normativa/leyes/Documents/Juridica/
LEY%201448%20DE%202011.pdf.

Santos, J. M. (2010). "Palabras del presidente Juan Manuel Santos en la presentación
de la Ley de Víctimas" [speech transcript]. Presidencia de la República de
Colombia, September 27. http://wsp.presidencia.gov.co/Prensa/2010/Septiembre/
Paginas/20100927_07.aspx.

Santos, J. M. (2011a). "Palabras del presidente de la República, Juan Manuel Santos
Calderón, en el acto de sanción de la Ley de Víctimas y de Restitución de Tierras"
[speech transcript]. Presidencia de la República de Colombia, June 10. http://wsp.
presidencia.gov.co/Prensa/2011/Junio/Paginas/20110610_07.aspx.

Santos, J. M. (2011b). "Palabras del presidente Juan Manuel Santos en la presentación
del Sector de la Inclusión Social y la Reconciliación" [speech transcript]. Presidencia de la República de Colombia, November 9. http://wsp.presidencia.gov.co/
Prensa/2011/Noviembre/Paginas/20111109_10.aspx.

4
Top-Level Follow-Up and Monitoring

The Fight against Poverty: A Presidential Commitment

In every government effort (among the many that an administration must take on to tackle a country's various problems), there is a subjective element that largely determines its success or failure: a president's commitment and leadership.

In my particular case, in my campaign and during the eight years I served as head of State, I identified certain priorities, which I conveyed to my ministers and the entire government team and monitored frequently. These included improving security and, to that end, ending an internal armed conflict with the Revolutionary Armed Forces of Colombia (FARC), a guerrilla army we had been at war with for over half a century; lowering unemployment; and, very importantly, reducing poverty. These last two priorities were framed within a more ambitious overall goal: seeking improved conditions for equity—in employment, health care, education, housing, basic utility services—for the most vulnerable Colombians.

Poverty reduction was a priority for me (as it should be for anyone in power), and I was convinced that it was feasible. With appropriate policies and concrete programs, we could substantially reduce poverty, which meant improving families' quality of life. What gave rise to that priority? A sense of empathy toward people experiencing poverty. This empathy grew every time I visited a population in some region of the country and saw what it meant for people to gain access to services they didn't have and that we take for granted in the cities, such as electricity, gas for cooking, drinking water, decent housing, or education for their children. Their lives were literally transformed, and their opportunities to have a fuller life multiplied.

One anecdote has stuck with me. When I was minister of finance, I authorized the money to provide a power plant to a very poor population in Colombia's Pacific region, which had never had electricity. When I went to officially turn it on, they welcomed me as if Jesus Christ had arrived because their lives had been profoundly changed. Now they could keep their food

The Battle Against Poverty. Juan Manuel Santos, Oxford University Press. © Juan Manuel Santos (2023).
DOI: 10.1093/oso/9780192885234.003.0005

cool, ward off the unbearable heat with fans, read at night, or watch soccer games on television.

The priority of the fight to reduce poverty became a public policy that had not only the president's backing but also his direct supervision. And that top-level leadership became a factor in this policy's success. Every minister understood that, regardless of their entrusted sector's performance, their work would also be assessed and recognized according to its contribution to the poverty-related targets. And they knew that the person directly supervising this policy was the president himself.

At the end of 2011, wrapping up my administration's first year, we had already begun implementing the Colombian Multidimensional Poverty Index (C-MPI) as a new poverty measure, we had included it in the National Development Plan, and we had established the social inclusion and reconciliation sector, led by the new Department for Social Prosperity (DPS in Spanish).

Now, it was time to use these new elements as public policy tools and optimize their use via coordination and monitoring mechanisms. These mechanisms would allow the president to evaluate, drive forward, and correct whatever was required so that the priority of the fight against poverty wouldn't remain on paper but would rather become a positive reality for millions of Colombians. There were two mechanisms: the Cross-Cutting Poverty and Inequality Roundtable and a dashboard to monitor the fulfillment of the sectoral poverty-related targets.

Development of the Coordination and Monitoring Mechanisms

No one disputes that, globally, one of the firms most recognized for its reliability and quality in strategic management consulting is the US company McKinsey & Company, founded in 1926 by James O. McKinsey, considered the father of management accounting. This firm has worked for over 25 years in Colombia, advising private-sector companies and public entities. It is at the vanguard of everything related to organization and methods.

Aligned with the priorities I had set for my administration, I decided to organize some monitoring roundtables on three specific topics: security, employment, and poverty. To establish and design them, we hired the services of McKinsey Colombia. At the time, it was directed by Luis Fernando Andrade, an expert engineer in organizational strategy and transformation projects. He had been part of the founding team of the firm's offices in São Paulo and Bogotá.

To create the Poverty Roundtable, the McKinsey analysts met with the National Planning Department (DNP in Spanish) experts who had worked to formulate and implement the C-MPI and who were already moving forward with designing different monitoring schemes. On behalf of the Office of the President, the person who coordinated all this work with McKinsey and the DNP was María Lorena Gutiérrez, the presidential advisor for good governance.

Why did we establish the Poverty Roundtable? When a new public policy is set, one that breaks away from the traditional way in which a priority issue—such as poverty—is being tackled, the policy's good performance depends on continuous and close supervision. When faced with a proposed change, every bureaucratic apparatus tends to go back to the traditional way of doing things, to the previous and familiar model. And we didn't want that to happen. That's why it was important to establish a coordination mechanism, led by the president himself, so that we could ensure that senior government officials remained committed to the new guidelines for the policy on poverty.

Why did we turn to a firm such as McKinsey to design and start up this mechanism? On the one hand, I believe in the advantage of using the best minds and the most effective tools—what we can call the "state of the art" in organizational matters—to streamline the State's operations. On the other hand, ministers, especially ministers at a high political level, have a natural tendency to create their own fiefdoms, doing what they believe is right for the sector they are responsible for, without coordinating with other ministries or government bodies. In the long run, this produces counterproductive results: it is similar to having a powerful carriage pulled by spirited horses, each one tugging in the opposite direction.

The issue of poverty is far too important to be subject to this kind of territorialism. Reducing poverty is a team effort, and playing to win is our unavoidable duty.

In order to ensure this teamwork and synchronize efforts, we created this coordinating body. In it, ministers defended their points of view, while also listening to others' views, until they reached agreements that would enable them to move forward to accomplish the government's priority objectives. At a high level, I promoted debate and allowed different opinions to surface. If an agreement was not reached naturally, I used my privilege as president to make the final decision, trying to bring the "defeated" minister into line with the defined policy. My responsibility, as a leader, was to turn differences into synergies, and we did so on many occasions in the implementation of the policy against poverty.

Initially, McKinsey's work to design and start up the Poverty Roundtable had two benefits. The first was that, hand in hand with the Office of the President and the DNP, the roundtable's composition and operations were clearly defined so that it would be an effective body for coordination, evaluation, decision-making, and the definition of commitments. The second benefit was that since McKinsey was an independent consulting firm, it had greater influence and represented greater impartiality than another government entity. That is how we succeeded in bringing together the various ministers and directors of entities at a roundtable in which they often had to sacrifice the interests of their respective sectors for the interests of the defined priority interest—in this case, poverty reduction.

Once the Cross-Cutting Poverty and Inequality Roundtable's composition and operations were defined, we needed a tool that we could use at this roundtable to monitor and evaluate each ministry or participating entity's commitments and objectives more effectively.

Invited by the Inter-American Development Bank, my advisor, María Lorena Gutiérrez, traveled to Washington to learn about and study various monitoring mechanisms. At the White House, they showed her the scorecards that had been implemented in Bill Clinton's administration, which used a traffic light system (green, yellow, and red) that had proved to be very useful for the Office of the President to monitor its priority policies. That is how she and I began a strategic planning effort with each minister. Between the end of 2010 and early 2011, I visited each ministry and received a report from the ministers—together with their deputy ministers, heads of planning, and other leadership staff—on their respective strategic plans and targets for the four-year period. Based on these visits, María Lorena and her team developed 16 dashboards—one per State sector—to be able to periodically review developments in each set target with each minister. A dashboard was also designed to analyze the performance of the 25 priorities I set as president, as well as, of course, a dashboard to define the progress and challenges in everything related to the fight against poverty.

The Cross-Cutting Poverty and Inequality Roundtable

Who composed the Poverty Roundtable, and how did it operate? As president, I led the roundtable, which included the heads of the main ministries and entities related to the issue. Their participation was nondelegable, meaning that ministers, not deputy ministers or any other representative, had to attend. In particular, the ministers of education, health, housing, agriculture, labor, and finance formed part of the roundtable, as did the directors of the National Administrative Department of Statistics (DANE in Spanish), the Colombian Family Welfare Institute, and the National Agency for Overcoming Extreme Poverty (ANSPE in Spanish). When the DPS was established and became fully operational, its director joined the roundtable. First the DNP, and later the DPS, served as the roundtable's technical secretariat.

The roundtable's main objective was the top-level coordination of the public policy against poverty, based on monitoring the performance of every C-MPI dimension and indicator. Therefore, the public official participants were the heads of the sectors directly related to the poverty reduction strategy on issues such as health, housing, food, employment, and education, and in charge of the government's main social programs, such as those focused on low-income families or children.

The roundtable met at least twice a year, notwithstanding the fact that it could be convened more frequently, as indeed we did on several occasions. The meeting in the first half of the year focused on analyzing the previous year's poverty figures as soon as the DANE produced them. These figures allowed us, with statistical rigor, to identify the progress and challenges in the poverty reduction targets that we had proposed. In the meeting during the second half of the year, and any other additional meetings held, we concentrated on monitoring the specific targets for each multidimensional poverty dimension (Angulo and Zavaleta, 2018).

They were dynamic meetings in which, based on incontrovertible data and facts, the government monitored the behavior of social indicators and made decisions to drive forward or correct whatever was deemed necessary. To me, they were extremely useful in every respect.

A concrete example can illustrate how the roundtable's deliberations affected policies. In one of the first meetings, an evaluation was conducted of the programs that the Ministry of Housing had designed to implement in the 2010–2014 period. The main program was the construction of major social housing projects in the country's big cities, which targeted low-income families with a mixture of cheap credit from the financial sector and State benefits. The DNP, based on the strategies proposed by each ministry in the National Development Plan, had run simulations that made it possible to determine how much each program contributed to the overall goal of poverty reduction. That was precisely the purpose of the C-MPI: for us to estimate how each sector contributed to this priority goal.

After running the simulations, the DNP concluded that these major housing projects in big cities contributed very little to reducing poverty since poverty was concentrated more in rural areas and among small populations in the country's regions. I remember a moment of tension at that roundtable meeting. While the DNP director demonstrated, with figures and projections, the housing projects' irrelevance to meeting our social targets, the minister of housing forcefully defended the program she had designed and was starting up. That is when a president, as a leader, has the responsibility to settle an issue and define a solution.

After each side presented its arguments and the experts were heard, I made the decision to change the priority of the housing policy so that it would stop focusing on cities and, instead, target the most remote and poorest regions in the country. Of course, the minister wasn't happy about this, but this was the essence of this coordination work: to drive forward what was working well and to correct what needs a change of course.

From that moment on, the Ministry of Housing concentrated on designing a policy with greater effect in the regions, and the Ministry of Agriculture did the same for the issue of rural housing. Right after my second presidential term began, we launched a revolutionary program to build 100,000 free homes for the poorest families in the country's most remote towns and regions—and when I say free, I mean absolutely free, without any kind of loan—and another 100,000 homes, also free, in rural areas for small-scale farmers.

Professor John Hammock, co-founder of the Oxford Poverty and Human Development Initiative (OPHI), was at the roundtable meeting in which these decisions were made. Later on, he told me that he was very impressed by this dynamic and that he uses it as an example in his talks or when he discusses the Multidimensional Poverty Index (MPI) in countries that have implemented it or are interested in doing so. "This is what has to happen with this index," Hammock asserts. "The MPI isn't just a measurement tool. It's a tool for governments to take action."

Professor Hammock and Professor Sabina Alkire have told me that the OPHI has learned much from Colombia's experience of implementing the MPI. In June 2015, a Multidimensional Poverty Peer Network meeting was held in Cartagena, and they were impressed by four ministers who participated in the event, presenting to the panel about how they used the C-MPI to evaluate the performance of education, employment, health, and housing programs. It became clear to them how each of these senior officials had internalized the importance of making progress on the goal of poverty reduction, how to use the MPI as an oversight tool, and the need to coordinate their actions with other ministers and with the government in general to be more effective.

The Poverty Roundtable proved to be a very appropriate coordination mechanism for optimizing social programs. Among other issues, in addition to retargeting housing policy and establishing the free housing program, the roundtable discussed redesigning the conditional transfer program Familias en Acción (Families in Action), which was renamed Más Familias en Acción (More Families in Action). It also discussed major obstacles to equality, such as the lack of access to education, which led to designing programs such as Ser Pilo Paga (Being Smart Pays Off), standardization of the school day, and free tuition for all students on official campuses from grade zero to eleven. Initiatives on creating jobs, reducing informal employment, improving health-care quality and coverage, and providing comprehensive early childhood care were also established. Chapter 5 will discuss several of these programs and their contribution to the priority goal of poverty reduction in more detail.

I highlight here, as a lesson learned, the importance of using the C-MPI—via the DNP creating simulated scenarios that determine each sectoral strategy's degree of contribution to the overall goal—to prescribe social policy. Through the Cross-Cutting Poverty and Inequality Roundtable, the senior officials who were members ended up understanding the need and advantage of coordinating efforts. And it wasn't just those officials. For me, as president, it was an opportunity to regularly review the performance of the different sectors against our poverty reduction targets and to make decisions that would lead to meeting these targets.

In a way, the roundtable became a forum for the most responsible and implementing parties of social policy to report back to the president. When we analyzed each ministry or entity's indicators, I'd ask them, "How is this progressing?" And, if no progress was reported, "Why isn't progress being made? What's missing? What do we have to fix?" For that same reason, as I noted earlier, I gave the decisive instruction that the ministers' presence at the roundtable was nondelegable since it was the head of each sector that had to answer for its accomplishments or shortcomings. This produced great coordination and, at the same time, administrative pressure so that they would make the necessary investments and do the necessary work. And the figures show that the coordination and pressure were effective.

The Poverty Roundtable met in different locations: a few times at the Casa de Nariño, other times at the offices of socially relevant public entities such as the National Training Service (SENA in Spanish), and other times in different regions of the country. At each meeting, we sought to invite guests who were world-class experts on the subject of poverty, members of the academic community, or representatives of international entities such as United Nations Development Programme (UNDP), the Food and Agriculture Organization (FAO), the International Organization for Migration (IOM), the World Bank, the Inter-American Development Bank (IDB), the Economic Commission for Latin America and the Caribbean (ECLAC), or the United States Agency for International Development (USAID). In this way, we enriched the debate with innovative ideas and also called on multilateral or foreign cooperation organizations to support our crusade for equality and against poverty.

At the end of each roundtable meeting, a press conference was called to inform the country about the poverty indicators (if we had a new report), their progress or setbacks, and the main decisions made.

The Dashboard

A fundamental element for the Poverty Roundtable's operations was the dashboard. As I mentioned, this was prepared by the Office of the Presidential Advisor for Good Governance, with support from McKinsey and the DNP experts.

The dashboard was the quintessential tool for measuring and evaluating results in the fight against poverty and inequality, as it allowed us to visualize, succinctly and graphically, the performance of each sector and its evolution toward the proposed targets.

The monitoring was conducted using four main statistical indicators: the monetary poverty index, the C-MPI, the Gini coefficient, and the number of families who overcame poverty within the social safety net known as Red Unidos (United Network).

When we analyzed the monetary poverty index, which is the traditional poverty measure according to each family's income, the minister of finance and the DNP director were the main spokesmen since this index mainly reflects macroeconomic policies. It was also compared with the results from the Employment Roundtable since level of employment largely determines each family's monetary income.

In the case of the Gini coefficient, which is the quintessential measure of inequality, we studied its performance at both national and regional levels and debated how to continue increasing the incomes of the poorest people to increasingly close the social gap. Initially, the ANSPE director was responsible for Red Unidos. After ANSPE's merger with the DPS in 2016, the DPS director gave the presentations on this program. In all cases, we relied on the technical information provided by the DANE.

Naturally, the indicator that proved to be the most useful for our evaluation of concrete advances in improving families' quality of life was the C-MPI. Not only did we review this index's changes, but we also differentiated advances, standstills, or setbacks in each of its five dimensions (household education conditions, conditions of children and youth, employment, health, and access to public utilities and housing conditions) and the 15 indicators into which these dimensions are subdivided.

Thus, the various ministers and entity directors answered to figures, not perceptions. They did so by using a system to benchmark progress against the official targets set by each sector in the National Development Plan. The microsimulations run by the DNP already made it possible to know the necessary pace of progress for each sector to meet the target at the end of the four-year period.[1]

The dashboard reflected the changes in each indicator by emulating the colors of a traffic light.[2] In each quarter, there had to be at least 25% progress toward the annual target. In this context, if quarterly progress was between 0% and 10%, that indicator's traffic light appeared red; if progress was between 10% and 25%, the traffic light turned yellow, and if progress was 25% or greater, it showed green.

This is how we identified, sector by sector, indicator by indicator, how different aspects of our social policy were moving forward. We're talking about concrete and measurable issues, such as educational achievement, literacy, school attendance, school lag, access to early childhood care, child labor, unemployment, informal employment, health insurance coverage, easy access to health services, provision of drinking water, waste collection and treatment, household floors and walls, and overcrowding. We had some defined targets for each indicator, and the traffic light system, previously prepared by the Office of the President and the DNP, served us as an instrument to detect strengths or identify aspects or programs that required correction or an additional push.

We not only reviewed these indicators nationally but also regionally, so that we could learn in which regions of the country we were making the best progress and in which there were lags requiring our response.[3]

---

[1] The DNP's "Guía para la construcción y análisis de indicadores" ("Guide to Develop and Analyze Indicators") mentions the importance of the dashboard and indicators in the Council of Ministers (DNP, 2018, p. 31).

[2] In recent years, the Fundación Paraguaya has developed an instrument called the "Poverty Stoplight" as a tool for individuals and families to assess various dimensions of poverty. For more information, see Cavanna (2019).

[3] The DNP also used the dashboard regionally to track and monitor poverty reduction in the country's different regions. For concrete examples, see the dashboards in the Caribbean region (DNP, 2016, p. 4), Atlántico, and Chocó (DNP, 2017, pp. 5–6).

I remember a deathly silence in the room when we introduced the dashboard at a Poverty Roundtable meeting. It was inevitably a moment of tension since each minister or entity director saw, in bright colors, a reflection of their programs' progress or standstill against the poverty targets. They had to answer for this—not only for their programs' performance against their sectoral targets but also for their contribution as a sector to the priority goal of reducing multidimensional poverty.

In essence, it was about achieving effective coordination and the greatest possible involvement of senior government officials in reaching a goal that was not exclusive to their sector but cross-cutting: to improve the quality of life of the most vulnerable Colombians in aspects that we could measure and monitor. Each year, as we will see in Chapter 5, the indicators in red became "alerts," and initiatives were launched to remove bottlenecks and accelerate progress toward the relevant targets.

A Memorable Meeting

There are many anecdotes about what happened internally at the Poverty Roundtable when the dashboard was introduced and about the way in which we made decisions at this top-level body for optimizing government social policy.

Of the various roundtable meetings, I remember, due to its special circumstances, one held on April 17, 2013, at a National Training Service (SENA) campus in Bogotá. This campus was, at the time, directed by Gina Parody, who I later appointed as minister of education. We met there because, a few weeks earlier, we had launched the Jóvenes en Acción (Youth in Action) program, through which we offered free technical education at that entity, in addition to monthly financial support, to thousands of low-income young people.

That day, we were accompanied by Professor John Hammock from the OPHI and the director of the newspaper *El País* from Spain, Javier Moreno, who had come to Colombia to do a news story on me. But the conditions surrounding the meeting were not the best. Rumors had arisen that we were going to privatize SENA—one of the many instances of fake news spread by the opposition and which never happened. While we were in the meeting, we began hearing rabble-rousing, shouts, and banging on the entrance doors. They were unionists and some SENA students protesting against the alleged privatization. The police controlled the situation, but we had to hold our meeting amid that external tension, in a closed room, which we didn't leave for something over three hours. My private secretary asked me, "What should we do?" And I responded, "We stay. Keep presenting the poverty indicators."

We had been in government for just over two-and-a-half years, and the results were very encouraging, showing how our shameful rates of poverty and inequality were decreasing. The monetary poverty index had dropped from 37.2% in 2010 to 32.7% in 2012, meaning that about 1.7 million Colombians had risen out of monetary poverty. In the same period, extreme monetary poverty had fallen from 12.3% to 10.4%, drawing us closer to our goal of bringing it down to a single-digit figure.[4] In the same period, multidimensional poverty had also decreased from 30.4% to 27%.[5]

In addition, we had achieved something exceptional: lowering the inequality index (Gini coefficient) from 0.560 in 2010 to 0.539 in 2012, a decrease that was mainly explained by income redistribution policies and, to a lesser extent, by the economy's growth. With this, we went from being the second most unequal country in Latin America and the Caribbean—only behind Haiti—to the seventh. Furthermore, we became the second country in the region that most reduced inequality and poverty between 2010 and 2012.

That day, amid the commotion and tension of the protests, we were able to give Colombia great news, which we continued to produce year after year: the country was steadily making headway in reducing poverty and inequality (*Semana*, 2013). Of course, Javier Moreno did not miss this opportunity and wrote a full feature in *El País* on this meeting's events, which he published on April 25, 2013.

To conclude his story, Moreno quoted some comments I made to him in the car as we were returning to the Casa de Nariño:

Now we're a normal country, not a disgraceful and shameful country with inequality. This is more important than taking out the FARC's number one and number two,[6] more important than a surplus. For me, this day is perhaps the most important one I've had in my 33 months of administration so far.

(Moreno, 2013)

---

[4] The data on monetary poverty and extreme monetary poverty corresponds to calculations using the Mission for the Splicing of Employment, Poverty, and Inequality Series (MESEP) methodology.

[5] The C-MPI data is calculated based on the 2005 census projections.

[6] Two results of operations that had taken place during my administration, in 2011 and 2010, respectively.

Conclusion

What we achieved with the Cross-Cutting Poverty and Inequality Roundtable and the dashboard was to make the most of statistical indicators, turning them into concrete actions. In other words, we managed to turn the C-MPI from being a multidimensional poverty measurement instrument into a very valuable tool for multisectoral public policy.[7]

It is worth noting that good ideas come to stay. Both the Poverty Roundtable and the dashboard, which we implemented in my administration, were continued under another name—now it is called the Equity Roundtable—by my successor's administration. Unfortunately, his four-year period did not see such positive results, which is only partly explained by the COVID-19 pandemic. Although the pandemic had direct and collateral effects that increased poverty in Colombia and worldwide, monetary poverty and inequality also increased because the president did not prioritize social matters and did not personally take on the issue.

The tools are there to continue fulfilling their mission. But it's not just about the tools. For them to function properly, they must be backed up by the head of state's leadership and the highest level of commitment.

Lesson 4
To Reach Priority Goals, Mindsets and Paradigms Must Be Shifted

During my career in public life, as the head of three ministries and then as president, I have understood that, beyond designing and implementing good government policies and programs, and beyond the tools used to put them into practice, there is an element that permeates everything and that is essential in the success or failure of what is undertaken: the human factor.

Personalities are complex and the job of a person who leads a team—and beyond that, a team of men and women with strong academic qualifications and long professional careers—consists, in large part, of knowing how to coordinate the agendas and egos of those team members.

The first change required for a government to achieve optimal results is a shift in mindsets and paradigms.

When I was minister of foreign trade in the early 1990s, I stepped into a newly created ministry and had to row against the current. President

---

[7] See Angulo and Zavaleta (2018, pp. 17–20).

Gaviria assigned me the responsibility of opening up the Colombian economy, an economy that had long been closed and protected by high tariffs against international competition. The opening was a 180-degree turn in the understanding of our trade and our economy. We did it through dialogue, persuasion, and consensus-building, not only with the country's businesspeople—accustomed to a scheme of benefits and protectionism that was no longer sustainable—but also with several of my Cabinet colleagues, who still advocated for keeping the old system. Then, I began to understand that, to change an organizational culture, meaning changing the way bureaucrats traditionally operate, you have to turn to compelling reasons and, moreover, conduct strict monitoring and supervision so that inertia does not return things to their previous state.

In my experience as minister of finance, between 2000 and 2002, I had to handle a different kind of challenge: preparing the national budget and distributing it among the various sectors during the worst economic crisis we had suffered since the Great Depression. If a finance minister should have anything, it is the capacity to take the pulse of their colleagues, who expect greater budget allocations for their policies and programs, and of politicians, who advocate for resources for their regions. In the end, everyone must give in for the greater overall interest (i.e. the interest of all citizens), which is reflected in each government's priorities.

I learned another great lesson from the nearly three years I spent as minister of defense because if any activity requires coordination and synergy, it is maintaining security and ultimately peace via the armed forces, especially if you are at war. When I took on the position in mid-2006, I encountered a reality that was damaging our ability to fight illegal armed groups: the jealousy that existed among the various forces that made up the military and between the military and the national police. Each force felt ownership over the intelligence information it collected and did not share it with the others. That had to change. With help from British (MI6), Israeli (Mossad), and US (Central Intelligence Agency) advisors, I redesigned our armed forces' intelligence system, creating an overall intelligence command that centralized all the information from the forces. It wasn't easy. I had to bring the generals into line more than once. But soon the facts demonstrated the new system's virtues. High-value targets, which, until then, had stayed out of our reach, began to fall one after the other. And so, the balance of power of the war in Colombia changed.

In a government, it is natural for every minister to want to make an impression and seek to work in favor of their entrusted sector. What we achieved with instruments such as the Poverty Roundtable and the dashboard was to create synergies around a common and priority goal, which was reducing poverty and inequality. The ministers understood that they were not only evaluated on their sectoral results but also on their contribution to the overall results in the fight against poverty.

Under presidential leadership, egos were tamed, there was a paradigm shift, and the results were swift.

References

Angulo, R. (2016). "Multidimensional poverty measurement in Colombia: What lessons can we learn?" *Dimensions, 1*, 11–14. https://mppn.org/wp-content/uploads/2016/10/DIMENSIONES_1_English_vs2_smallest-1.pdf.

Angulo, R., and Zavaleta, D. (2017a). "In brief: Roundtable and dashboard for the reduction of poverty in Colombia." *Dimensions, 2*, 10–12. https://mppn.org/wp-content/uploads/2017/02/Dimensions_2_ENG_vs3_online_pages.pdf.

Angulo, R., and Zavaleta, D. (2017b). "National roundtable and dashboard for poverty reduction in Colombia." University of Oxford, OPHI Briefing 45. https://ophi.org.uk/national-roundtable-dashboard-for-poverty-reduction-in-colombia.

Angulo, R., and Zavaleta, D. (2018). "Colombia: Building scenarios for setting MPI goals: From multidimensional measurement to multisector public policy." *Dimensions, 5*, 17–20. https://mppn.org/wp-content/uploads/2018/11/Dimensions-Nov-2018._EN_webversion.pdf.

Cavanna, J. (2019). "El semáforo de eliminación de la pobreza." Banco de Desarrollo de América Latina. Fundación Paraguaya. https://scioteca.caf.com/bitstream/handle/123456789/1495/El_Sem%C3%A1foro_de_Eliminaci%C3%B3n_de_la_Pobreza.pdf?sequence=1.

Departamento Nacional de Planeación. (2016). "Informe de seguimiento territorial 2014–2018 región Caribe." Departamento Nacional de Planeación.

Departamento Nacional de Planeación. (2017). "Pobreza monetaria y multidimensional departamental: Necesidad de políticas públicas diferenciadas." Panorámica Regional (3rd edn). https://colaboracion.dnp.gov.co/CDT/Prensa/Publicaciones/Publicaci%c3%b3n%20Ipm%20deptal.pdf.

Departamento Nacional de Planeación. (2018). "Guía para la construcción y análisis de indicadores." https://colaboracion.dnp.gov.co/CDT/Sinergia/Documentos/Guia_para_elaborar_Indicadores.pdf.

Drèze, J., and Sen, A. (1989). *Hunger and public action*. Clarendon Press.

Mitra, S. (2013). "Towards a multidimensional measure of governance." *Social Indicators Research, 112*(2), 477–496. https://doi.org/10.1007/s11205-013-0256-4.

Moreno, J. (2013). "Tengo mis líneas rojas y sé qué ceder; de ahí no me mueve nadie." El País, April 25. https://elpais.com/internacional/2013/04/25/actualidad/1366919348_421582.html.

Semana. (2013). "En pobreza, salimos de un vergonzoso puesto." Semana, April 17. https://www.semana.com/economia/articulo/en-pobreza-salimos-vergonzoso-puesto/340414-3.

5
Policies and Programs to Reduce Multidimensional Poverty

Challenges Revealed by the Multidimensional Poverty Index

One of the main goals of measuring the Multidimensional Poverty Index (MPI) is to improve the targeting of social investment to make it more efficient and reach the sectors with the greatest impact on poverty reduction. As a result of analyzing changes in the different dimensions and indicators that make up the Colombian Multidimensional Poverty Index (C-MPI), which we did at the Poverty Roundtable meetings, we defined which sectors or programs we should emphasize and which we should change or correct to be more effective. The dashboard traffic light not only signaled progress on the different targets but also produced alerts that served to redirect our efforts and resources toward responding to concrete needs in various areas.

The correlation between alerts and public policy illustrates how we took into account, with the utmost seriousness, the challenges that analyzing the C-MPI revealed to us.

In 2011, alerts were sounded on the first and second C-MPI dimensions, related to household education conditions—in particular, low educational attainment—and child-care conditions, especially in the early childhood phase from birth to five years of age. In response, free education programs and a comprehensive early childhood protection program, called "De Cero a Siempre" ("From Zero to Forever"), were designed and set in motion.

In 2012, the alert was about the C-MPI's fifth dimension, corresponding to housing conditions. That is when we decided to scale down the major social housing projects in the big cities and focus our energy and budget on a program with much greater impact on the fight against poverty: a program to build at least 100,000 free homes for the poorest families in the country, not only in the cities but also in municipalities with small populations.

In 2013, at the roundtable, we detected that the pace of reducing monetary poverty had slowed and that a large gap persisted between the living

The Battle Against Poverty. Juan Manuel Santos, Oxford University Press. © Juan Manuel Santos (2023).
DOI: 10.1093/oso/9780192885234.003.0006

conditions of urban populations and those of rural farming populations. We decided to redesign the Families in Action conditional assistance program and increase its coverage in rural areas.

In 2014, the C-MPI alerted us to difficulties in social mobility, largely produced by youth unemployment. In response, we established a free technical education program at the National Training Service (SENA in Spanish) with financial support for students' livelihoods, called, as mentioned earlier, Youth in Action. As a result of this program, more than 430,000 young people, who were finishing secondary school with no options to continue their studies or to have a well-paid job, found the possibility to receive education and training in technical, technological, and professional fields, not only at SENA but also at various higher-education institutions in the country.

In 2015, alerts surfaced on issues such as Colombian children's nutritional conditions and the lack of coordination in rural housing programs. With the Department for Social Prosperity (DPS in Spanish), we worked to strengthen the National Food Security Plan with various projects throughout the country. Regarding housing for rural farmers, with the Ministry of Agriculture, we launched a program to build or improve more than 100,000 houses in rural areas, in addition to the 100,000 in the free housing program run by the Ministry of Housing, which focused on municipal seats.

In 2016, we registered an alert about an accomplishment of ours two years back, in 2014. In 2014, the so-called established middle class—the class considered not at risk of falling back into poverty—had surpassed the population living in poverty. In other words, there were more people in the middle class than people in poverty. This was a first. Nevertheless, the monitoring figures in the following year gave us cause for concern: the so-called emerging middle class—which includes the people who have just risen out of poverty—was highly vulnerable to falling back into it. To ward off this vulnerability, we implemented policies and projects specifically aimed at protecting the incomes and living conditions of people who belonged to the emerging middle class, in areas such as employment, housing credit, and access to higher education.

In 2017, the roundtable's alerts indicated an increasing trend of inequality in the gap between the incomes of those who earn the least and those who earn the most in the country. In response, we launched programs with an emphasis on rural areas to support the most vulnerable families and improve their earning capacity, not only by creating jobs but also by supporting small enterprises.

Between 2017 and 2018, we identified a challenge about implementing the ambitious social agenda laid out in the peace agreement that we had signed with the Revolutionary Armed Forces of Colombia (FARC) in November 2016. In response, we brought bills before Congress that would put this agreement into practice, and we succeeded in giving the agreement a constitutional status that would prevent it from being disregarded by future administrations.[1]

These are just a few examples. Of course, with such a comprehensive measure as the C-MPI, all of the social protection dimensions demanded our response and led us to carry out concrete actions, which ultimately resulted in lowering multidimensional poverty in the country.

In the rest of this chapter, I will address in more detail three particular areas that saw substantial progress due to these innovative policies and programs that we established based on the needs detected at the Poverty Roundtable. These areas are early childhood care and education, decent housing for families, and expanded high-quality health care for the vast majority of Colombians.

Comprehensive Early Childhood Care

February 21, 2011 was a day filled with hope. On that day, in the Plaza de Armas outside the Casa de Nariño (the presidential palace), we launched the National Strategy for Comprehensive Early Childhood Care, "De Cero a Siempre" ("From Zero to Forever"). My wife, María Clemencia, was the visible head of this initiative, leading it with support from María Cristina Trujillo, the presidential advisor for early childhood until the end of my administration and who had worked for me before. The chairs of private foundations and representatives from the Inter-American Development Bank and other multilateral institutions joined us, in addition to a very special guest: James J. Heckman, the Henry Schultz Distinguished Service Professor of Economics at the University of Chicago, a 2000 Nobel laureate in economics and an expert in the economics of human development.

---

[1] Among other laws that constitutionally protected the peace agreement with the FARC, Legislative Act 2 of May 11, 2017, issued by Congress, incorporated a transitory article into the Constitution. The second paragraph of this article establishes that:

> State institutions and authorities must comply in good faith with what is established by the Final Agreement. Consequently, the actions of every State organ or authority, the normative development of the Final Agreement, and its interpretation and implementation shall be coherent with and fully responsive to what has been agreed, preserving the contents, commitments, spirit, and principles of the Final Agreement.

This provision applies "until the end of three complete presidential terms after the signing of the Final Agreement," that is, until 2030.

Why had we invited Professor Heckman? In his globally recognized work, carried out in an interdisciplinary manner with psychologists, neuroscientists, statisticians, and other economists, he stated that early childhood development from birth until five years of age "directly influences economic, health and social outcomes for individuals and society" (Heckman, 2013).

According to Professor Heckman, these first years of life, when each person's cognitive and character skills are built, are the best time "to shape productivity." Promoting these skills early on contributes to creating productive citizens. Very importantly, targeting support to children who are in vulnerable and low-income environments substantially reduces social costs, meaning "costs to taxpayers [avoided] by investing in developmental opportunities for at-risk children." And not only that; Professor Heckman demonstrated that "investing in early childhood education is a cost-effective strategy for promoting economic growth" (Heckman, 2013).

So, joined by this very distinguished guest, we introduced a strategy in the country that was bound to produce short-, medium-, and long-term transformations by improving these future citizens' education and productivity, reducing social costs and inequalities (which begin in early childhood), and driving economic growth.

That day, I began my speech with the following words: "What issue can be more important for a nation than its children's well-being? Guaranteeing their rights today is not only a constitutional mandate, but also a clear political decision of our administration" (Santos, 2011).

And it was. We put this strategy at the core of our social policy, aiming to instate it permanently. To this end, we promoted a law in Congress—Law 1804 of August 2, 2016—which made this strategy a State policy that future administrations are compelled to continue to implement and promote.

When I began my administration, we had more than five million children aged 0–5 in Colombia; of these, 56% lived in poverty and, much more seriously, 23% lived in extreme poverty. There was a universe of approximately 2.5 million children aged 0–5 in a situation of vulnerability, of whom only 151,312 were served by early education programs in 2011. We set ourselves a target of increasing this served population tenfold, and in 2018, we already had 1,467,492 children in this age group receiving comprehensive care.[2]

How did we do it? We united various State entities' scattered efforts for young children and called upon the private sector, social and community

---

[2] See Single System of Information on Children (SUIN in Spanish), cited in Santos (2020, pp. 148–149, 364).

organizations, academia, and international cooperation agencies as partners. In this way, the various actors—working on aspects such as health, care, education, nutrition, identity, and rights protection—coordinated smoothly with each other in a system focused on comprehensive care for the youngest children.

For this purpose, an Intersectoral Commission for Comprehensive Early Childhood Care was formed, coordinated by the Office of the President itself and composed of entities such as the Ministries of Education, Health, Housing, and Culture, as well as the National Planning Department (DNP in Spanish), the Colombian Family Welfare Institute, the Victims' Unit, and the Administrative Department (now the Ministry) of Sports.

Public investment in early childhood increased from 1.1 trillion pesos (about 237 million dollars) in 2010 to 4.2 trillion pesos (about 907 million dollars) in 2017.[3] It practically quadrupled. This was complemented by resources from public–private partnerships, as various companies and foundations enthusiastically joined the campaign. An example of this support was the Fundación Éxito, the social arm of a leading supermarket chain in Colombia, which led, and continues to lead, an initiative to eradicate chronic malnutrition in children.

What does comprehensive care consist of? When we say that nearly 1.5 million children aged 0–5 received comprehensive care in 2018, this means that they are children who are registered at birth, enrolled in the health system, and fully immunized. They have growth and development check-ups as well as nutritional assessment and monitoring. Finally, they attend an early education institution with qualified staff, where they receive 70% of their nutritional needs and have access to books or cultural content specifically designed for the first years of life. Furthermore, families receive training on providing appropriate care and raising their children. All these children, when they grow up and become citizens, will have the cognitive, physical, and emotional tools to be healthy individuals in every sense, who are able to build a more equitable and happy society.

To cover shortages in high-quality early childhood care, 274 new child development centers were delivered and equipped across the entire country, and 150,000 people were properly trained to provide comprehensive care for children. I cannot thank my wife María Clemencia enough for her support

---

[3] The exchange rate of the US dollar against the Colombian peso has been very volatile in 2022 and the beginning of 2023, fluctuating between COP 3,700 and a little more than COP 5,000. For practical purposes, and as a rough reference for readers, this book uses a rate of COP 4,632 per USD 1, which was the representative market exchange rate on January 31, 2023. Whenever we talk about pesos, we mean Colombian pesos, and whenever we talk about dollars, we mean US dollars.

and commitment in this endeavor. Every night, she would ask me what I'd done that day for "her" children.

As Professor Heckman rightly said, "The highest rate of return in early childhood development comes from investing as early as possible, from birth through age five, in disadvantaged families. Starting at age three or four is too little too late [. . .] Efforts should focus on the first years for the greatest efficiency and effectiveness."[4]

With the National Strategy for Comprehensive Early Childhood Care, "From Zero to Forever," we took an enormous step in the social protection of the country's poorest people,[5] not only to care for the needs of the youngest and most vulnerable children but also because we had faith in investing in productive human beings who will positively contribute to society and be able to escape the vicious cycle of violence and poverty.[6]

Notably, the C-MPI, which we officially adopted in August 2011, incorporated this early childhood strategy, which was already an ongoing initiative; the index also helped to ensure continued response and monitoring of the strategy. Access to early childhood care services became one of the four indicators comprising the C-MPI's second dimension, "Conditions of children and youth."

Access to Education: Free Primary and Secondary Education and Other Areas of Progress

I have always said that, in public administration, love is shown in the budget. It is not enough to develop lofty policies or design innovative programs if policies and programs are not backed by sufficient resources to make them a reality.

For a long time in Colombia, the State sector that received the largest share of the budget was the defense and security sector. This is understandable in a country like ours, which has had to confront violence by guerrilla armies, paramilitary groups, and drug-trafficking organizations for decades, and which—going even further back—was the Latin American nation with the most civil wars in the nineteenth century. Nevertheless, it is clear that the origin of this violence often lies in the lack of opportunities for people. Children and young people with access to education, health care, housing, and

---

[4] Cited in Santos (2020, p. 151).

[5] The analysis by García et al. (2014) shows a gradual reduction in multidimensional poverty in children and adolescents.

[6] To learn more about the "From Zero to Forever" strategy's impact evaluations, see Bernal et al. (2017) and DNP (2018).

basic utility services, as well as employment opportunities once they have finished their studies, are at less risk of swelling the ranks of subversive or criminal groups.

In my administration, thinking about that, we deliberately decided to substantially increase the education sector's budget, to such an extent that, in 2015, for the first time in the country's history, it was the most-funded sector within the national budget. This is still the case today. Between 2010 and 2018, investment in education increased by around 80%, growing from 20.8 trillion pesos (about 4.5 billion dollars) to 37.4 trillion pesos (about 8.1 billion dollars).[7]

I proposed a goal for the country, which I still believe we can reach: to make Colombia the most educated country in Latin America by 2025. The first step to achieve this, which we identified at the Poverty Roundtable, was to ensure that all school-age children did, in fact, attend school and that their families' limited economic resources did not pose an obstacle to do so. In 2011, we made education free at all public schools for primary, lower secondary, and upper secondary education, that is, from grade 0 to grade 11, before beginning higher education, whether at a university or technical institution.[8] As a result of this measure, since 2011, more than 8 million students attend school without paying a single peso for their education. This was a fundamental step.

Additionally, to ensure students' classroom attendance and reduce dropout, we strengthened the School Meals Plan, which guarantees more than six million daily food rations for children. With these two measures, free education and school meals, we succeeded in reducing school dropout rates significantly. Many kids were sent to school just because they were being fed. While the dropout rate during the school year was 4.8% in 2010, it had fallen to 3% in 2018.[9]

Adding to these two measures, another factor favored the reduction in school dropout: the maintenance and expansion of the Families in Action program, under the DPS's responsibility, which I have referred to in previous chapters. This program—inspired by the Progresa program launched by Mexican President Ernesto Zedillo (a good friend; we are now both part of The Elders, a group of independent global leaders working together for peace, justice, human rights, and a sustainable planet) during his time—began

---

[7] See "Budget execution reports"—Ministry of National Education, cited in Santos (2020, pp. 146–146, 364).

[8] In Colombia, primary and secondary education encompasses 11 years of schooling: primary school (grades 1–5), lower secondary school (grades 6–9), and upper secondary school (grades 10–11).

[9] See Ministry of National Education, cited in Santos (2020, pp. 152–153, 365).

operating in 2000, when I was minister of finance, and we strengthened it during my administration. It consists of bimonthly direct cash transfers to the poorest families in the country. The transfers are only made if these families fulfill two conditions: they send their school-age children to school and take their children to regular nutrition check-ups. Using this carrot approach encourages parents, knowing that the program ensures additional income for their families, to keep their children in school instead of pulling them out to work.

The Families in Action program was raised to the level of a national law (Law 1532 of June 7, 2012), which means that it became a State policy, to prevent the bad, very Latin American habit of wiping the slate clean and starting over with different programs every time a new administration takes office— the "Adam complex," we call it. Unfortunately, my successor tried to do this with ours. To his credit, he continued this program not only because it was the law but also because he came to understand the benefits. Beginning in 2013, we increased the monetary incentive in the poorest areas of the country, particularly with respect to education, providing a higher amount for each additional year a family sent their child to school in order to strengthen school attendance until the last grade: eleventh grade. At the end of my administration, this large-scale program had benefited 2.5 million families, many of whom moved forward on their path out of poverty.[10]

However, producing real social transformation not only requires children's school attendance but also the provision of high-quality education. In this regard, we identified serious inequality between private school students and public school students. While students at private schools attended schools with an eight-hour or longer school day, students at public schools, due to the shortage of school infrastructure, had to be split into two shorter school days with four to six hours of classes: a morning session for some and an afternoon or evening session for others.

Beginning in 2015, we began to correct this situation, implementing school days of the same length at more than 1,700 public schools. Consequently, children received more hours of schooling. Of course, this entailed an additional challenge: building more classrooms to increase schools' physical capacity to take on more students. In just over three years, we built or began building 19,000 new classrooms and contracted construction services for another 11,000, for a total of more than 30,000. This covered 60% of the educational infrastructure shortage in the country, even though later on we

---

[10] The impact evaluation of this program conducted by Arteaga, Trujillo, and Gómez (2019) shows the positive effects of the program's implementation on poverty reduction.

unfortunately discovered significant corruption in the building of this new infrastructure. Additionally, we devoted ourselves to supplying schools with the highest-quality educational materials. We delivered more than 50 million free textbooks that facilitated teachers' work and students' learning.

Beyond this, because learning depends on much more than textbooks and brick buildings, we worked on something I consider fundamental: human talent. Thanks to a program we named "Todos a Aprender" ("Let's All Learn") that we launched in 2012 with the then Minister of Education, María Fernanda Campo, we dedicated ourselves to innovatively strengthening our teachers' skills, using a peer-to-peer methodology inspired by a project developed by the University of Liverpool. How did we do this? We selected the best teachers in the country, whose students showed the best results, and we sent them to support, as mentors, teachers at the schools with the lowest educational achievement rates, many of which were in the poorest and most remote regions.

As part of this solidarity and sharing work, thousands of mentors distributed themselves across the entire country to communicate their knowledge and educational experiences with their colleagues. Specifically, we concentrated on improving language and mathematics lessons. It didn't take long for the results to show, with a substantial improvement in rural schools that took part in the program. This was another way to close gaps—in this case, educational gaps between rural and urban populations.

Even before our country joined the Organization for Economic Cooperation and Development (OECD) in 2018, one of my initial objectives, after years of efforts to adapt our policies and procedures to the high standards of this group of countries recognized for their good economic and governance practices, we had been measuring our students' performance to compare it with OECD members' performance on the recognized Programme for International Student Assessment (PISA) tests. I have always been convinced that it is better to compare yourself with the best because this habit—striving for excellence and not matching mediocre standards—is the only way to reach the best goals.

Although our students still lag far behind students in the world's most developed countries, important advances, especially in mathematics and science, were noted between 2009 and 2018. In the words of OECD Secretary General Ángel Gurría, "These improvements are the result of a long transformation in the Colombian education system." He added, "Colombia's real success has been its ability to increase the number of enrolled students and, at the same time, improve their performance" (Ministerio de Educación Nacional, 2016).

With primary and secondary education guaranteed for children from lower-income families, the next step was to offer them alternatives to continue their education at universities or technical institutes. Between 2010 and 2018, the percentage of young people accessing higher education increased from 37.1% to 52%.[11] This increase came with a very special characteristic, which is encouraging in the goal to close the social gap: 60% of the new students came from low-income homes.

One program in particular, which we worked on and launched with Minister of Education, Gina Parody (who, inspired by a similar program in Australia, conceived the idea), at the beginning of my second term in office, helped make a difference. I'm referring to the "Ser Pilo Paga" ("Being Smart Pays Off") program.[12] Through it, young people who came from the lowest income brackets and had the best academic qualifications were given the opportunity to pursue—completely free of charge—a degree program of their interest at a higher education institution of their choosing, public or private. In the four years that the program lasted (unfortunately, my successor canceled it and swapped it out for another program with less reach), more than 40,000 young people who had never dreamed of reaching elite universities began studying at the best academic institutions.

This has led to many positive consequences. On the one hand, each young person benefiting from the program became an agent of transformation and social mobility within their own family and environment. On the other hand, universities benefited from having students of great academic merit on their campuses, who also enriched the student and teacher environment, improving diversity and inclusion. Even now, at different events, I run into young people who are successful professionals today and who tell me that they were able to study and achieve their dreams and their families' dreams thanks to the opportunity the "Being Smart Pays Off" program gave them.[13]

Education, undoubtedly, is the most powerful tool for not only individual but also social transformation. For that reason, we gave it an enormous push between 2010 and 2018, confident that in advancing educational coverage and quality, especially for the most vulnerable Colombians and those in rural areas, we were advancing toward our higher goals: poverty reduction and greater equity.

---

[11] See Single System of Information on Higher Education (SNIES in Spanish)—Ministry of National Education, cited in Santos (2020, pp. 156–157, 365–366).

[12] In Colombia, the adjective *pilo* (smart) refers to a judicious, disciplined, and diligent person.

[13] The impact evaluation conducted by the Centro Nacional de Consultoría and the Centro de Estudios de Desarrollo Económico (2016) showed a significant closure of gaps in access to higher education.

As with access to early childhood care services, several of these aspects of children and young people's education are also essential components of the C-MPI. In this sense, we have been able to monitor them with accurate and comparable data by analyzing the behavior of this index and discussing these aspects at the Poverty Roundtable. Two indicators in particular, school attendance and no school lag, which are part of the C-MPI's second dimension, "Conditions of children and youth," provided the government with input to promote the abovementioned education policy and programs.

In Colombia, it hasn't been necessary to develop a child-specific MPI since indicators addressing early childhood care and assistance to educational centers, in addition to an indicator on child labor, are already incorporated into the C-MPI. Consequently, these indicators have contributed to public policy decisions that lead to improving conditions for children's growth and education.

Access to Decent Housing for the Poorest

I mentioned before that one of the first concrete conclusions that came out of a Poverty Roundtable meeting and the analysis of different programs' impact on the targets to reduce the C-MPI had to do with housing. At one of those meetings, we concluded that the major social housing program—subsidized housing with cheap credit for poor families—in large cities did not particularly help our poverty reduction goal as the housing deficit was more concentrated among small populations and rural areas in the country.

Thinking about this, we designed a revolutionary program that had never been attempted before in Colombia: to build and hand over thousands of absolutely free homes to the poorest families in the country, meaning those whose incomes did not even allow them to access a subsidized credit in the financial sector. The microsimulations run by the DNP indicated that a program of this nature would have a very significant impact on reducing the C-MPI.

In total, between 2010 and 2018, 1.7 million homes were built, or were being built, in our country, representing an improvement in the living standards of more than 5 million Colombians. Of these homes, 60% received some kind of co-financing from the government through different programs and subsidies. These subsidies, in the case of the free housing program for the poorest people, reached 100% of the home's value, meaning zero costs for the beneficiaries. As a result, the quantitative housing deficit in the country dropped from 12.3% of households without adequate housing in 2005 to 5% in 2018.[14]

The free housing program that we initiated in 2012 was possible thanks to a revolutionary housing law passed in June of that same year, which we pushed forward with then Minister of Housing, Germán Vargas, who later became my vice-president. Through the program, 130,000 housing units—30,000 more than the initial target—were delivered to low-income families across the country, particularly in the smallest and most remote municipalities. They were decent homes, with all basic utilities and good-quality common areas. Each family even received, along with the keys to their new home, a small collection of books to start their family library and an allowance to buy a computer and have a broadband connection.

More than a housing program, what we put in place was a comprehensive package of measures to benefit the poorest families. By just delivering one of these homes, we were satisfying several of the indicators that make up the C-MPI since the homes were not just a roof to sleep under: they had an entire set of additional goods and services—utilities, an internet connection, the necessary number of rooms for sheltering a family, good-quality walls and floors—that truly provided dignified conditions for people to live in.

This program positively affected all five indicators that make up the C-MPI's fifth dimension, "Access to public utilities and housing conditions": access to an improved water source, elimination of sewer waste, adequate floors, adequate external walls, and no critical overcrowding. And not only these indicators but also others outside of the index, such as an internet connection, for example, were also impacted.

In allocating the homes, we considered three possible criteria: the families were very poor, lacked access to bank credit, or were victims of the internal armed conflict or affected by natural disasters. There was a draw to select families from among those meeting one of these criteria; in reality, we didn't have enough homes to meet the full demand, but it was a first and very important step. It should be clarified that the 130,000 free homes that we built with the Ministry of Housing in the municipal seats were in addition to the rural homes that were delivered or improved by the Ministry of Agriculture. These ultimately reached more than 170,000, exceeding the initial target, which was also to build or improve 100,000 rural homes. In total, more than 300,000 homes—under the free scheme—transformed the lives of 300,000 families.

---

[14] See National Administrative Department of Statistics (DANE in Spanish), 2005 and 2018 censuses, cited in Santos (2020, pp. 132–133, 363.

If anything made me happy within the daily hustle and bustle of government work, it was visiting the country's different towns and cities to deliver the housing projects to humble Colombians who hadn't ever dreamed of having a house of their own. They were very emotional ceremonies, with a mingling of gratitude and tears from both beneficiaries and the government team itself.

There was no shortage of voices questioning the benefits of the free housing program for the poorest people. They said it was a moral hazard, too welfare-oriented, that it ran the risk of new owners selling their homes for money instead of living in them, or that they wouldn't be able to keep them up or pay for utility services. Many of these concerns were taken into account. For example, this program's beneficiaries had to remain in the home for at least ten years after it was given to them, and they could not sell it during this time frame.[15] They were exempt from notarial and registration fees when obtaining their property deeds, and they would pay the lowest-rate utility services, corresponding to socio-economic stratum one,[16] for the first ten years. Apart from that, both the national government and regional governments prioritized resources to build and provide housing projects with collective public facilities, such as parks, community halls, sports facilities, or health centers. The truth is that the free homes were more than a gift; they became an opportunity to bring dignity to thousands of families' lives. The families understood it in this way and have taken care of their homes, even expanding and improving them, and they have learned to responsibly live a dream they had not dared to dream of before: having a home of their own.

Other critics said that the homes were very small or suboptimal quality. To quiet them, I decided to spend a night at one of the apartments in a residential complex that we had delivered in Valledupar, in the country's Caribbean region, a city famous for being the capital of *vallenato* music. I wanted to personally confirm that the apartment was in good condition, that it had water, that the shower and sanitation services worked, and that it was possible to sleep well. That created a commotion in this small city. No one expected the president, who had come to deliver homes to the poorest of the poor, to spend a night in one of them. I slept very well because the apartment was truly comfortable. The next morning, I woke up and sat on a small footstool to read the local newspaper, wearing my shorts-and-t-shirt pajamas. The presidential

---

[15] The new Housing and Habitat Law (Law 2079 of 2021) shortened the term to be able to sell the property received in the free housing program from ten to five years.

[16] In Colombia, a system of socio-economic stratification influences the value of utility bills. In this system, residential dwellings are classified into six strata (low to high economic status), typically divided by neighborhoods, and the first three strata are charged subsidized rates.

photographer did not miss the opportunity to take a picture of me, which went viral. Colombians, with their caustic humor, entertained themselves saying that they'd taken a picture of me in my underwear while I was in the bathroom. It's an occupational hazard, but I learned that I had to be careful about how and when they took my photo to avoid any misunderstandings or give my critics free ammunition.

The truth is that the free housing program was created with a goal, which it fully met: to contribute decisively to eradicating extreme poverty. Hundreds of thousands of families who lived in the most precarious conditions found, in a home of their own, a new future.[17]

This was complemented by important progress on the coverage of basic utility services and internet connections, in part explained by the high number of homes built or improved. During 8 years of government, 6.3 million Colombians were able to have drinking water in their homes for the first time, and 7 million accessed basic sanitation services, meaning sewage and waste management services. Another 9 million people transitioned from having propane gas cylinders or cooking on wood stoves—with the damage this does to residents' health and to the environment due to deforestation—to having in-home, modern, and affordable natural gas connections (Santos, 2020, p. 136).

If there is one service that has become essential in the twenty-first century, characterized by progress and expanded communications and connectivity, it is the internet. When we began our administration, there were 280 municipalities—of Colombia's total 1,102—with access to fiber-optic backbone networks and 2.8 million internet connections. Eight years later, in 2018, every municipality in the country had a fiber-optic connection, and we had around 28 million broadband connections, representing a tenfold increase (Santos, 2020, pp. 138–139). While in 2003, only 5.5% of households had access to the internet, by 2018 more than half of Colombian families, 52.7%, had this service in their homes.[18]

Here, I've mostly referred to the programs that helped to lift the poorest families out of poverty, but it should also be noted that with other programs (subsidizing the interest rate on housing financing, for example), we were able to support thousands of middle-class families to fulfill their dream of having a home of their own.

---

[17] Camacho-González, Caputo-Leyva, and Sánchez-Torres (2022) highlight this program's important impacts on beneficiaries, not only in terms of access to housing but also in access to utility services, working conditions, women's workforce participation, and income generation.

[18] See DANE, 2003–2018 National Quality of Life Survey (ECV in Spanish), cited in Santos (2020, pp. 141, 363–364).

What took place between 2010 and 2018 was a true revolution in housing and basic utility services, which not only increased Colombians' quality of life but also helped to improve employment figures and economic performance, given the reactivation of the construction sector, which is one of the most labor-intensive sectors.

Coverage and Equity in Access to Health Care

If there is one area in which Colombia can show fundamental progress in this century, and particularly since 2010, it is in protecting the health of its population. Not only did we reach universal coverage (more than 95% of the population has some form of health insurance), but we also enshrined health as a fundamental right and unified mandatory health plans so there would no longer be first- and second-class patients.

With political will, we worked to improve the C-MPI's fourth dimension, health, in its two indicators: health insurance coverage and access to health services in case of need. In fact, the health sector was the one that most contributed to reducing multidimensional poverty in Colombia between 2010 and 2016. Of the 12.6 percentage point decrease in that period,[19] 4 percentage points are attributable to the improvement in the population's access to health services and growing financial health insurance (Ministerio de Salud y Protección Social, 2017).

In at least three indicators measured by the World Health Organization (WHO), our country today has outstanding performance—without ignoring, of course, that many problems and shortcomings remain. Let's take a look. The first indicator considered by the WHO is the percentage of the population with access to health services. In this respect, we increased coverage from 29.2% in 1995 to 55.6% in 2000, 93.6% in 2010, and 95.2% in 2019.[20]

The second indicator is the number of treatments included in patients' health care. In this respect, Colombia has one of the most generous systems. In addition, there is a legal mechanism—established by the 1991 Constitution—called *acción de tutela* (a legal action to protect fundamental rights). As a result, any person may request a procedure or a medical prescription, even if these are not included in the mandatory health plans. The vast majority of these legal actions are decided quickly in favor of the petitioners,

---

[19]   Comparing data calculated based on the 2005 General Population and Housing Census projections.
[20]   See DANE and the Ministry of Health, cited in Santos (2020, pp. 184–185, 366–367).

which guarantees their right to health, although it entails a high economic cost for the State.

The third indicator taken into account by the WHO is the percentage of families' income that must be spent on health expenditures. In this respect, we have one of the lowest percentages in the world, meaning that households do not carry a very heavy burden since the State mostly covers these expenditures. According to a study published by the British journal *The Lancet*, out-of-pocket spending on health in Colombia—that is, the share of health expenditures that Colombian families must make out of their pockets—was 20.6% of total health spending in 2016, which implies that about 80% is covered by public resources. In comparison, average out-of-pocket spending on health stood at 42.7% in Latin America (Universidad Icesi, 2019).

Despite the Colombian health system's good level of coverage, when I took office as president, I found a panorama of terrible inequity. There are two systems of health coverage in our country. One is the contributive system, which includes all people who allocate a percentage of their income or wages to have health coverage for themselves and their families. This system mostly includes formal workers and self-employed people with high incomes, who have the economic capacity to contribute to the health system. The second system is the subsidized system, which covers informal workers, self-employed people, or unemployed people who do not have the capacity to contribute to the health system.

At the time, there were more and better compulsory health plan benefits for the contributory scheme than for the subsidized scheme. In other words, low-income people who did not have formal employment and were affiliated to the subsidized scheme did not have access to the same treatments, procedures, and medications as those affiliated to the contributory scheme. To give specific examples, procedures as urgent and sensitive as an operation to remove gallstones or as necessary as anti-reflux surgery were not included in the subsidized scheme's plan of benefits. Patients, often overwhelmed by pain and at risk of dying, had to take legal action, such as filing a *tutela*, or bring their case before special committees that could authorize the procedure.

Aware of this, and taking on an enormous fiscal effort, in 2012, I issued a decree unifying the benefits of the contributory and subsidized schemes. From then on, there were no more first- and second-class patients, which meant an important step forward in our goal of reaching greater equality among Colombians. Today, all people with health insurance—that is, more than 95% of the population—have the same plan of benefits, regardless of the scheme they belong to.

This was a fundamental step, but we lacked something else to achieve the equality we aspired to in the health system. According to Article 49 of the Political Constitution of Colombia:

> Public health and environmental sanitation are public services for which the State is responsible. All individuals are guaranteed access to services that promote, protect, and restore health. It is the responsibility of the State to organize, direct, and regulate the provision of health services to the inhabitants and sanitation in accordance with the principles of efficiency, universality, and solidarity.
>
> (Political Constitution of Colombia, 2021, p. 35)

This supreme law of the land enshrines the right to health, but for this right to be fully put into practice, Congress had to adopt a statutory law to regulate it. More than 20 years had passed since the Constitution's adoption, and this still hadn't been done. So, with Minister of Health, Alejandro Gaviria, we proposed pushing this law forward in the legislature. The Statutory Health Law was successfully approved, thus enshrining health as a fundamental autonomous right, guaranteeing health-care provision, regulating health care, and establishing protection mechanisms.

This law—which I signed on February 16, 2015—was the first statutory law in Colombia to regulate a fundamental social right, making it absolutely clear that access to health services must be comprehensive, equal for all, and free from administrative obstacles. Navi Pillay, the then United Nations High Commissioner for Human Rights, who was in Colombia in July 2013 when Congress approved this law, praised it as a pioneering accomplishment in the world.

One example sheds light on how the Statutory Health Law changed the provision of this essential service. Before the law was passed, there was a common practice in health institutions that the media graphically called "the carousel of death." If a person was experiencing a medical emergency and went to an emergency room at the closest clinic, hospital, or health center, they were often denied admission because the health company from the contributory or subsidized scheme to which they were affiliated did not have an agreement with the institution. So, the patient would be sent to another medical center, and then to another, until—not infrequently—they ended up dying.

The issuance of the Statutory Health Law made it clear that every entity providing health services has the inescapable obligation to respond, care for, and provide the necessary emergency services to anyone who comes in with a medical emergency, without even asking for the company or scheme they are affiliated to, much less if they have the financial resources to pay for any treatment.

Thousands of lives have been saved as a result of this provision. And not only that; the Statutory Health Law strengthened price controls for medicines throughout the supply chain until the final consumer. The Ministry of Health took on this task. Pharmaceutical prices had been deregulated in 2006, and in some cases, they had reached exorbitant levels that jeopardized the system's sustainability and led to significant expenditure for families. It was a titanic battle against pharmaceutical companies, and we had to fight it in Colombia and abroad. Today, more than 1,800 medications have a regulated price, which has saved the health system more than 5.5 trillion pesos (about 1.2 billion dollars). The price of hepatitis C medications alone dropped by 80%, and the cost of medications for heart problems, psychosis, epilepsy, ocular hypertension, mycosis, and even contraceptives decreased in similar proportions.[21]

Other statistics reflect the progress of health programs, especially for the protection of children and women living in poverty. The country's maternal mortality rate (deaths per 100,000 live births) declined from 71.6 in 2010 to 45.3 in 2018;[22] the infant mortality rate (deaths of children under one year of age per 1,000 live births) went from 12.7 in 2010 to 11.3 in 2018.[23] Furthermore, and very importantly because it is a factor that helps perpetuate poverty, we reached the lowest adolescent pregnancy rate as of that point in the century. While 20.5% of adolescent girls (women aged 15–19) were mothers or pregnant in 2005, this rate had dropped to 17.4% in 2015.[24]

Without a doubt, adolescent girls prematurely becoming mothers has economic and social implications. These young women see their plans to study and to work thwarted; they leave the school system early and, if they begin working, receive insufficient wages. How did we achieve this important reduction? We strengthened and provided specific health services for young people and adolescents, adopted a cross-sectoral approach to the problem, and facilitated access to contraceptive methods.

In short: the work to improve health services and Colombians' health conditions in the second decade of this century had several facets. Not only did we maintain universal health coverage, but we also eliminated the differences between the treatment of patients with greater and fewer resources. We unified the contributory and subsidized schemes' benefit plans. We promoted

---

[21] See *El Tiempo*, cited in Santos (2020, pp. 196–197, 368).
[22] See Ministry of Health and Social Protection, cited in Santos (2020, pp. 186–187, 367).
[23] See Ministry of Health and Social Protection, cited in Santos (2020, pp. 188–189, 367).
[24] See ICBF, cited in Santos (2020, pp. 190–191, 367).

the Statutory Health Law, which made health an enforceable fundamental right and ended the "carousel of death." And we controlled the prices of hundreds of medications. Not for nothing did the OECD state the following in its 2016 report on Colombia's health system:

> Colombia offers a remarkable example of rapid progress toward universal health coverage that deserves to be better known internationally. It has achieved financial protection against excessive health care costs for almost all citizens, as well as an equal basket of services for those in and out of formal employment.
>
> (OECD, 2016, p. 11)

Lesson 5
Innovative Solutions for Chronic Problems

This chapter's lesson shows how, in the face of chronic problems, concrete and quick-acting solutions that make a difference can be devised.

At the Poverty Roundtable, year after year, we identified sectors that required deeper intervention because they were lagging behind, demonstrating situations of inequity or lack of social service coverage, or negatively influencing our goal to reduce multidimensional poverty.

A middle-income country like Colombia, with an internal conflict and violence that have been going on for decades and with large gaps between the development of its urban and rural areas, faces enormous challenges that require creating and implementing innovative solutions. These solutions do not just bear fruit in the short term; often, they are seeds whose results will be seen decades later.

This is the case with comprehensive early childhood care and protection. All the care we give to our children from the time of their birth to five years of age, when their brain and abilities are being formed, will lead to benefits for them and for society as a whole when these little ones become good, productive citizens who create well-being and advocate for peace. In this regard, the "From Zero to Forever" program, transformed into a State policy, is a solid investment in the future.

Something similar can be asserted about the progress in access to education. When we decreed free primary and secondary education at all public schools, when we built thousands of new classrooms for students to have the same number of hours in the school day, when we provided economic assistance to the poorest families so they would send their children to school, or when we succeeded in thousands of the best students in the country from low-income households going to the best universities to study their chosen degree, we made an enormous investment in Colombia's future.

Education is the greatest tool for transforming a society. If I am proud of anything, it is of having given the education sector, for the first time in our history, the largest share of the national budget. Every investment in educating human talent is returned several times over to the society that makes it.

Nothing is more important for a household than the possibility of having a decent home, ideally of its own. We realized that it wasn't enough to provide subsidies for purchasing a house or to subsidize the interest rate of real estate loans when hundreds of thousands of the poorest families, in the most distant corners of the country, didn't have the remotest possibility of being considered eligible for credit in the financial system.

If we wanted to truly influence the extreme poverty in which these families were living, we had to produce a program that would not only give them access to housing but also transform and bring dignity to their lives. The free urban and rural housing program, which provided more than 300,000 fully subsidized homes to the poorest Colombian families, revolutionized the lives of hundreds of thousands of Colombians who today live in a pleasant, safe environment, with access to household utility services and the internet, and with common areas that encourage sports and healthy social interactions.

Health care—an issue that remains fraught with shortcomings and exclusions, even in the richest and most powerful nations, such as the United States—also demands will, coordination, and imagination to make substantive improvements. Fiscal and political costs must be taken on, as President Barack Obama did in his time when he pushed forward, against all odds, the Affordable Care Act. We did the same in Colombia when we promoted the Statutory Health Law, unified health benefit plans, and controlled the price of hundreds of medications, facing the powerful lobby of multinational pharmaceutical companies.

As the popular saying goes, "Big problems call for big solutions." My conclusion is that, with political will, leadership, and moral sense, it is possible to move toward a more just and equitable society.

References

Arteaga, X., Trujillo, C., and Gómez, L. (2019). "Evaluación de impacto Familias en Acción." Departamento Nacional de Planeación, Documentos Dirección de Seguimiento y Evaluación de Políticas Públicas, October. https://colaboracion.

dnp.gov.co/CDT/Sinergia/Documentos/Evaluacion_Impacto_FEA_Informe_
Resultado.pdf.

Bernal, R., Ramírez, S., and Arias, L. (2017). "Impactos de la estrategia "De Cero
a Siempre" sobre el desarrollo integral de los niños y niñas en primera infancia." Universidad de Los Andes and Instituto de Bienestar Familiar, December 13. https://www.icbf.gov.co/system/files/evaluacion_de_impacto_de_cero_a_
siempre_-_elca_uniandes_2017_1.pdf.

Camacho-González, A., Caputo-Leyva, J., and Sánchez-Torres, F. (2022). "'Un nuevo
comienzo': El impacto del Programa Vivienda Gratuita sobre la calidad de vida
de los hogares beneficiarios." Facultad de Economía, Universidad de Los Andes,
Centro de Estudios sobre Desarrollo Económico Documento No. 10. https://
repositorio.uniandes.edu.co/handle/1992/56981.

Centro Nacional de Consultoría, and Centro de Estudios sobre Desarrollo
Económico. (2016). "Evaluación de impacto del Programa Ser Pilo Paga.
Informe de resultado del levantamiento de línea de base, evaluación de
impacto de corto plazo y tercera entrega de la documentación de las bases
de datos." Facultad de Economía, Universidad de Los Andes, Departamento Nacional de Planeación. https://colaboracion.dnp.gov.co/CDT/Sinergia/
Documentos/InformeFinalSerPiloPaga.pdf.

DNP (Departamento Nacional de Planeación). (2018). "De Cero a Siempre: Informe
de resultados de la evaluación y tercera entrega de la documentación de la base de
datos de la evaluación." Econometría . . . Sistemas Especializados de Información.
https://colaboracion.dnp.gov.co/CDT/Sinergia/Documentos/Evaluacion_De_
Cero_a_siempre_Documento.pdf.

García, S., Ritterbusch, A., Bautista, E., Mosquera, J., and Martín, T. (2014).
"Análisis de la pobreza multidimensional en niños, niñas y adolescentes en Colombia: Metodología y principales resultados." Escuela de Gobierno Alberto Lleras
Camargo, Universidad de Los Andes, Documento de trabajo No. 8. https://
repositorio.uniandes.edu.co/handle/1992/8489?show=full.

Heckman, J. J. (2013). "Invest in early childhood development: Reduce deficits,
strengthen the economy." The Heckman Equation. https://heckmanequation.org/
www/assets/2013/07/F_HeckmanDeficitPieceCUSTOM-Generic_052714-3-1.
pdf.

Ministerio de Educación Nacional. (2016). "Colombia es el sexto sistema educativo
que más rápido ha mejorado entre los países de PISA 2015." Organisation for Economic Co-operation and Development, December 7. https://www.mineducacion.
gov.co/1780/w3-article-358730.html?_noredirect=1.

Ministerio de Salud y Protección Social. (2017). "Sector salud, el que más contribuyó
a reducción de la pobreza" [press release], March 23. https://www.minsalud.gov.
co/Paginas/Sector-salud-el-que-mas-contribuyo-a-reduccion-de-pobreza.aspx.

OECD (Organisation for Economic Co-operation and Development). (2016). "OECD reviews of health systems: Colombia 2016." https://read.oecd-ilibrary.org/ social-issues-migration-health/oecd-reviews-of-health-systems-colombia-2015_ 9789264248908-en#page1.

Political Constitution of Colombia. (2021). "Corte Constitucional de Colombia." https://www.corteconstitucional.gov.co/english/Constitucio%CC%81n%20en% 20Ingle%CC%81s.pdf.

Santos, J. M. (2011). "Palabras del presidente Juan Manuel Santos en la presentación de la Estrategia Nacional de Atención Integral a la Primera Infancia 'De Cero a Siempre'" [speech transcript]. Presidencia de la República de Colombia, February 11. http://wsp.presidencia.gov.co/Prensa/2011/Febrero/Paginas/20110221_04. aspx.

Santos, J. M. (2020). *Un mensaje optimista para un mundo en crisis*. Editorial Planeta Colombiana.

Universidad Icesi. (2019). "Gasto de bolsillo en salud de los colombianos es de los más bajos del mundo revela estudio de *The Lancet*" [press release], May 31. https://www.icesi.edu.co/unicesi/todas-las-noticias/5266-gasto-de-bolsillo-en-salud-de-los-colombianos-es-de-los-mas-bajos-del-mundo-revela-estudio-de-the-lancet.

6
Fieldwork

"Planting Hope"

Red Unidos: An Enormous Social Army

How can State services reach the poorest of the poor, those who live in remote rural settlements or in communities in the mountains surrounding the big cities, those who still do not have access to the internet and information from the media? This is one of the great challenges of any government, especially in a country like Colombia, where 14.4% of the population was living in extreme poverty in 2009.

During my administration, we managed to cut this percentage in half—to 7.2%—by 2018.[1] In total, around 3.6 million Colombians rose out of extreme poverty in the decade from 2008 to 2018 (DNP, 2019, p. 8). It was a spectacular achievement but not a lasting one. Unfortunately, the COVID-19 pandemic and a social policy that was not strong enough to curb its effects pushed us back into a level of poverty we had already overcome. By 2020, the percentage of Colombians in extreme poverty had climbed to 13.6%.[2]

The challenge of extreme poverty continues to be a priority. Therefore, it is worth analyzing in more detail a strategy aimed at the poorest of the poor, which we have already mentioned: the United Network for Overcoming Extreme Poverty, better known as Red Unidos.

In 2011, when we established the administrative social inclusion and reconciliation sector, we included in it an agency born from the former Office of the Presidential Advisor for Social Prosperity: the National Agency for Overcoming Extreme Poverty (ANSPE in Spanish). The ANSPE was entrusted with coordinating government actions to lift hundreds of thousands of families out of poverty. This agency, which merged with the Administrative Department for Social Prosperity (DPS in Spanish) in 2016, was tasked with

---

[1] The data on extreme monetary poverty corresponds to calculations with the Mission for the Splicing of Employment, Poverty, and Inequality Series (MESEP) methodology.
[2] Percentage also calculated with the MESEP methodology.

The Battle Against Poverty. Juan Manuel Santos, Oxford University Press. © Juan Manuel Santos (2023). DOI: 10.1093/oso/9780192885234.003.0007

managing Red Unidos, a strategy based on Red Juntos (Together Network), which had been established in 2007.[3]

Red Unidos coordinated efforts by the various State entities with social responsibilities to reach the greatest number of families living in extreme poverty—those who have the lowest scores in the System for the Identification of Potential Social Program Beneficiaries (SISBEN in Spanish)—or families registered in the National Victims Registry who have been displaced from their territories due to the internal armed conflict. This strategy delivers neither cash nor in-kind assistance; rather, it involves assessing the conditions of the poorest and most vulnerable families, explaining to them and advising them on how to improve these conditions, and supporting them on their path out of extreme poverty. Red Unidos aimed to support 1.5 million families across the country. At the end of my administration, we had reached nearly 1.1 million of them. However, something even more important happened: 365,000 families supported by this strategy rose out of extreme poverty.

How was this support provided? It was provided by a group of caseworkers: men and women who travel to even the most remote locations of the country to find these families, get to know them, determine their needs, and advise them on accessing State social services. I called these caseworkers my "social army" because that's what they were: more than 10,000 civil servants committed to their work, identified by a blue vest and hat with the Red Unidos logo, who hiked mountains, crossed rivers, traveled along rural roads, went into poor neighborhoods, and surpassed all barriers to reach the families most in need.

To select these caseworkers, the DPS put out public employment announcements. Then, it trained them with ongoing support from other national entities, municipal mayors' offices, and departmental governor's offices, which also organized training and information sessions for these civil servants to have greater knowledge of the government social programs they offered to beneficiary families, including both national and regional services.

When these caseworkers arrived at a household, the first thing they did was to survey the head of household—who, very often, is a woman—about 45 basic achievements in 9 dimensions of human development defined by Red Unidos as intervention areas: income and employment, livability, access to banking services and savings, nutrition, family dynamics, health, identification, access to justice, and education. Each of these dimensions is broken

---

[3] To learn about Red Unidos's first years of operations, see the report by Steiner, Acosta, and Vásquez (2010).

down into basic achievements, which are the minimum conditions that each family must meet to improve its situation in each dimension. By collecting this information, the caseworkers identified a household's socio-economic conditions and established its priority needs.

The dimensions and achievements that are part of the survey and the follow-up work have been revised to correlate with the Colombian Multi-dimensional Poverty Index (C-MPI) dimensions and indicators and with the Extreme Monetary Poverty Index. In this way, Red Unidos's targeted objectives align with the goals to reduce both multidimensional and monetary poverty that are set out in the National Development Plan.

The next step, after conducting the survey, was to establish a joint work plan so that the supported family could access the available goods and services in their municipalities in order to improve their quality of life. For example, if they met the requirements for conditional cash assistance from the Families in Action program, they would receive information on how and where they could enroll. This was also the case with other programs, such as Jóvenes en Acción (Youth in Action) for financial assistance to low-income students, Colombia Mayor (Older Colombia) with monetary support for older adults who do not have a pension or who live in extreme poverty, "De Cero a Siempre" ("From Zero to Forever") for comprehensive early childhood care, and initiatives to facilitate employment or support for small enterprises. At the time (my successor's administration discontinued them), it also included programs such as the free housing program or the "Ser Pilo Paga" ("Being Smart Pays Off") program, which we have already discussed extensively.

It was not just a survey or a one-time visit.[4] After the first visit, the caseworker would establish a personalized follow-up plan with the poor or vulnerable family and conduct periodic visits to check on their progress and help them overcome any obstacles they ran into until the family reached the outlined goal: rising out of extreme poverty. Through its social army, what Red Unidos used to do and, in a way, still does was to "ground" social policy, turning documents and good intentions into action in the very place where policy can be effectively implemented.

This is a clear example of a multisectoral policy integrated at the individual level. And its success laid precisely in this integration. Household deprivations cannot be treated in an isolated fashion since they are interwoven, and, similarly, government response must be comprehensive and all-encompassing, bringing together all State social services. In general,

---

[4] To see the details of this support, I recommend reviewing the case of Red Unidos support to families in Dagua, Valle del Cauca (Echeverry, 2014).

governments expect individuals in poverty to seek out and apply for programs for which they are eligible by themselves, going from one entity to the next. With Red Unidos, our goal was to reverse this direction so that the government would be the one seeking out low-income families, informing them about potentially beneficial programs, and advising and supporting them in their process to sign up and on their whole journey to rise out of extreme poverty.

Red Unidos is present in all municipalities of Colombia. The DPS, in charge of operating it, has incorporated a differential approach that considers the distinctive features of each family's needs, according to their urban or rural environment or their identity as members of ethnic communities.[5] In the case that families belong to ethnic communities, work is carried out in their respective collective territories, whether these are Indigenous reservations or lands allocated to Black communities, strengthening their collective capacities to improve their living conditions. In cities, work is concentrated in the neighborhoods or districts most affected by poverty.

Above all, this strategy has been a major coordination effort. National government entities involved in Red Unidos focus their resources on offering services to beneficiary families. There is also a degree of coordination with mayors, especially in municipalities with very high extreme poverty rates. Importantly, social services were managed in a complementary way with the private sector and international cooperation so that resources allocated to help vulnerable communities would serve to improve the living conditions of families involved in the program, whose most pressing needs are clearly identified.

As we did with the strategy for comprehensive early childhood care, "From Zero to Forever," and with the conditional cash assistance program, Families in Action, we also made the United Network for Overcoming Extreme Poverty (Red Unidos) into a national law—Law 1785 of June 21, 2016—to ensure its continuity.[6] This strategy, as a core, cross-cutting component of State social policy, has provided, and continues to provide, a coordinated and personalized response to the multidimensional problem of extreme poverty.

Indeed, Article 8 of the abovementioned law establishes that national entities must guarantee the preferential access of the households included in Red Unidos to State social services directly or indirectly related to the C-MPI

---

[5] See Bonilla and Torres (2018) and Econometría et al. (2012).

[6] There are many examples of laws that we drove forward to institutionalize social policies or, better yet, to make them into State policies. These include Law 1448 of 2011 (Victims and Land Restitution Law), Law 1532 of 2012 (Families in Action), Law 1751 of 2015 (Statutory Health Law), Law 1785 of 2016 ("Red Unidos Strategy"), and Law 1804 of 2016 ("Zero to Forever Strategy for Early Childhood").

dimensions (Law 1785 of 2016). In this way, the C-MPI proves its new usefulness by becoming an indicator and guide to determine the services to which
Red Unidos facilitates access.

Caseworkers for a Day

From the first weeks of my term, when the strategy was still called Red
Juntos, we realized the importance of spearheading this program to raise
awareness on the best way to support families to rise out of extreme poverty.
We focused on raising awareness among State officials, from ministers, governors, and mayors to middle managers at the various entities as well as
private-sector leaders and representatives of multilateral organizations or
countries interested in supporting us with international cooperation.

In October 2010, we held the first "Caseworker for a Day" event in Cartagena, aimed precisely at providing government officials—including myself
as president—with the opportunity to learn closely about Red Juntos's operations and to visit and survey beneficiary families. That day, I appointed myself
as a caseworker. Since then, on several occasions, I have had the opportunity to travel to the poorest areas in different cities or regions of the country,
putting on my blue vest and carrying out my role as another member of the
most noble of armies possible: the social army.

Many of these field visits were conducted as part of the "Caseworker
for a Day" initiative organized by the DPS. Not only members of the central government but also local authorities—governors, mayors, and their
cabinets—and the private sector were invited because we knew this was the
way to make traditional sectoral interventions into a joint effort to overcome
extreme poverty.

On several occasions, I carried out this work with all my ministers. As the
president and cabinet, we arrived in the most marginalized neighborhoods of
various cities in the country, and, joined by DPS officials, we conducted the
survey to evaluate each household's living conditions. It was a true "reality
check," which we all appreciated in the end. These work visits made it easier
to align all the government sectors with the priority to fight poverty, and each
sector contributed to the cause with more enthusiasm and knowledge.

We often brought private-sector executives or representatives of international organizations along to raise greater awareness of this social problem
and call for their support. Overcoming prejudices and even fears, men and
women with political or economic power had the unique opportunity to visit
marginalized areas and learn about poverty firsthand. It wasn't easy for many

of them, who had to overcome cultural or social constraints, but the feedback they gave us in the end was always positive.

One of the most rewarding experiences was when, at the end of February 2012, we took, 39 chief executive officers (CEOs) from the country's main companies to the eighteenth district of Cali, one of the poorest areas in this vibrant city in southwest Colombia, so that they could experience being a caseworker for a day.

Without a doubt, the day left a mark on the participants. Joined by the DPS director, we visited 44 families, saw their homes, and filled out the surveys on their living conditions. Many of the men and women who directed large corporations—such as Alpina, Telefónica, Pacific Rubiales, Unilever, Belcorp, Harinera del Valle, Colombina, Carvajal, and Manuelita, most of them listed on the stock exchange—had contact, perhaps for the first time, with the daily life of a family living in extreme poverty. This motivated them to deepen their companies' corporate social responsibility work and participate in public–private partnerships aimed at improving the living conditions of the poorest Colombian families.

This visit, the simple act of putting them in touch with a reality they know about but have not seen on the ground, was a very effective way to commit the private sector to the government priority of fighting extreme poverty and to familiarize it with the concept of multidimensional poverty. There is a great deal of talk about poverty; the virtue of this work was putting a name and face to it. They were no longer statistics but real people with needs and dreams.

Julián Jaramillo, the president of Alpina, an important dairy company, described the experience as "tremendously interesting" and especially highlighted "our potential to make an impact through unified, not dispersed projects" (DPS, 2012).

Ronald Pantin, president in Colombia of the Canadian oil company Pacific Rubiales Energy, emphasized that, in this program, "you see that things are going to reach the people and families most in need." He concluded, "If we all come together, the private sector and the public sector, surely we're going to succeed in lifting these people out of extreme poverty" (DPS, 2012).

Alfonso Gómez, president of Grupo Telefónica—the Spanish telecommunications emporium—in Colombia, said, "Without a doubt, the public sector and private sector are working on developing many important efforts. The idea is for us to begin working together more to be able to comprehensively attack the problem of extreme poverty" (Ramírez, 2012).

These testimonies attest to the importance of promoting more direct contact between people with public or private responsibilities and families living in extreme poverty as well as with government programs to improve this situation. Initiatives such as "Caseworker for a Day" encouraged synergies in the government and the private sector's work for vulnerable populations, and all of this led to good results.

A Heartening Example

As I said before, we have to put a name and face to poverty if we want to fully understand it. We've talked about the way in which different policies, initiatives, and programs have favorably impacted the country's poorest population, but it is always more illuminating when we can add a personal story to the numbers, one that shows us in practice how State actions can reach the areas most in need.

At the end of my administration, the DPS published a booklet with the main social achievements, which it titled *Legado para la Prosperidad* (*Legacy for Prosperity*). The text begins with a phrase that summarizes our priority well: "It has been eight years of the only war that was worth it: the war on poverty" (DPS, 2018, p. 7).

The booklet contains the story of Valeriano Domínguez and his family (DPS, 2018, pp. 64–70), one of hundreds of thousands of stories that illustrate how a family's life can be transformed with sensitive and well-designed policies and programs.

Valeriano was a farmer who lived with his loved ones in a rural settlement in the municipality of La Cruz, in the department of Nariño, in the southwest region of Colombia. One day in 2001, his cousin visited him, joined by a young man whom the guerrillas forcibly took away. Valeriano, who was a community leader in his settlement, interceded on behalf of his guest, even though he was a stranger. The guerrillas told him they'd taken the young man because he was an informant from the army. What is certain is that, from then on, they kept an eye on Valeriano and began to follow him, until a neighbor warned him that he had better leave town to save his life. Valeriano fled to Pasto, the capital of Nariño. A month later, after registering himself as a displaced person in the National Victims Registry and receiving his first round of humanitarian assistance, he returned to pick up his family: his wife Luz Dary, his daughter, and his little granddaughter.

His plot of land was left abandoned, like so many plots in Colombia that thousands and thousands of rural farmers have had to leave behind to escape violence and threats from illegal armed groups. Later on, Valeriano found out that the young man who had been held by the guerrillas had been found dead, with signs of torture. Any possibility of returning to his land vanished with that news.

"Truthfully, I felt awful," Valeriano says, "I'd left everything behind and had nothing here. No one who knew me. In the settlement, where I'm from and where we lived, we used to grow vegetables, plants; my wife also had a business selling sausage-topped French fries on the weekends. That's how we worked."

Now, with his family in Pasto, he began the struggle to find a place to live and paid work to cover his family's expenses. Together with a brother-in-law, he rented a piece of land and adapted it as a parking lot. Valeriano built a plank house with a provisional roof right there. Things were improving, but it was very hard work, day and night with no rest, in very precarious living conditions, in which they survived for several years. The house had a dirt floor and only one room, where they cooked and slept.

"One day," Valeriano continues telling his story, "a young woman in a blue vest showed up, talking about Red Unidos. She said she was conducting a survey. I told her we weren't from there, that we had been displaced. 'Exactly,' she replied. 'The Red Unidos strategy is for people like you. Let's talk because this is going to help you.'"

The young caseworker who visited them was named Sandra Paz. Remembering her visit, Valeriano's partner Luz Dary says, "I think that was the moment in which life started to get better for us, although at first we didn't realize it or believe in it much."

She goes on to talk about the caseworker's work: "She really helped us with the changes, providing us with information, guiding us, encouraging us, answering any questions we had about the paperwork. Planting hope in us, which we needed."

The caseworker visited the Domínguez home, surveyed them about the 45 basic achievements, and proposed they apply for a free home through the Ministry of Housing program. And they did. They participated in a first draw, in which 860 homes were awarded, but they didn't get one. Time passed, and with the caseworker's continued support, they signed up for another draw. This time, they won one of the free homes.

Today, Valeriano, his wife, his daughter, and his granddaughter live in Pasto in decent conditions, in an apartment that is part of two housing developments made up of 45 brightly colored towers and 1,508 apartments. They left the overcrowding, dirt floor, and lack of basic utility services behind, as did their new neighbors: more than 1,500 families who were victims displaced by the armed conflict or families affected by rainy season floods or relocated from high-risk areas.

A new caseworker took over supporting Valeriano's household, which in 2018—when the DPS booklet was written—was already close to being promoted, that is, moving from being a family in extreme poverty to a family en route to the middle class. Seventeen years after their displacement, the Domínguez family had a home of their own, connected to all basic utility services, and enough income to live decently. Valeriano worked at his mechanic shop, while Luz Dary took care of the home, helped look after her granddaughter, and sold perfumes by catalog. Their daughter had a job that allowed her to save up some money and was preparing to resume her university studies in accounting.

With guidance from the Red Unidos caseworkers, they followed the path to join the hundreds of thousands of families that have overcome extreme poverty in Colombia, and especially in Pasto, a medium-sized city in the country where multidimensional poverty fell from 28.1% in 2010 to 11.4% in 2017.

Valeriano finishes his story with this: "They haven't left us weapons to defend ourselves, but keys to open the future for our children with good messages, not with problems. We have to leave the problems behind, back there. Here, we have to make another life, start over."

Lesson 6
The Fight against Poverty Is Everyone's Work

If the experience of the United Network for Overcoming Extreme Poverty has demonstrated anything, it is the need to involve the greatest number of social actors in joint and coordinated work so that more families improve their living conditions, in every sense. In other words, it shed light on the importance of stimulating empathy in government officials, executives at private companies, and representatives of international organizations in the face of the phenomenon of poverty.

The fight against poverty is not exclusively the work of the national government, regional governments, or other State entities. Naturally, it requires clear leadership from those who hold power, as well as innovative public policies and well-structured programs, but none of this is enough without the overall support of society, including the private sector and international cooperation.

Part of the success of the strategy to fight poverty lies in the national government's ability to call upon other actors to work in the same direction. The private sector is usually looking for the best way to make social investments that benefit the communities where its factories or operations are located.

This is part of what is now called corporate social responsibility. In addition, companies' executives and shareholders understand something pragmatic that goes beyond altruistic considerations and is purely economic: the more families rise out of poverty, the more consumers with purchasing power to acquire products and services there will be. In other words, reducing poverty is a win–win for society and the private sector.

With experiences such as "Caseworker for a Day," the presidents of several of the most important companies in the country, after putting on their blue vests and visiting dozens of households in extreme poverty, became more directly and confidently involved in the various sectoral or cross-cutting programs for poverty reduction. As one of them told me, after the community work session, "Here I've found a way to measure the return on the funds we dedicate to social responsibility. As businesspeople, we like to measure the return. Perhaps it's not about profits, but in any case, it's important for us to know where our resources are going and how they're being used." In fact, many started to use the Multidimensional Poverty Index in their own companies.

Something similar takes place with Cabinet ministers or regional leaders. The experience of having direct contact with extreme poverty on the ground helped us to align them within the overall strategy to reduce multidimensional poverty. Each governor or mayor has their own priorities, but once we included them in the Red Unidos initiative, they found a way to adapt their priorities to the needs of their respective populations and the social services offered by the national government.

Working with local administrations is essential. For example, on the issue of housing, we created partnerships to build social housing projects in their municipalities. Mayors will always want a project of this kind to benefit their local residents. Consequently, they often provided the land for building the homes or the connections to basic utility services—a national-regional partnership that benefited those most in need.

The conclusion is clear: the national government cannot do it alone. Coordinated work with departments and municipalities, with support from the private sector and international cooperation, is the best guarantee of efficiency, transparency, and effectiveness in implementing policies and programs to overcome poverty.

Stimulating various public and private actors' empathy with low-income families' real situation—on the ground—led to two additional benefits: their intrinsic motivation to contribute to combating poverty and the creation of a kind of ethos and energy to optimize work in solidarity with the people and communities that most need support.

References

Angulo, R., Díaz, Y., and Pardo, R. (2011). "Índice de Pobreza Multidimensional para Colombia (IPM-Colombia) 1997–2010." Departamento Nacional de Planeación, Archivos de Economía No. 382. https://colaboracion.dnp.gov.co/cdt/estudios%20econmicos/382.pdf.

Becerra, L. L. (2019). "Las cifras de pobreza se redujeron casi a la mitad en la última década." La República, December 20. https://www.larepublica.co/especiales/especial-de-la-decada-2019/las-cifras-de-pobreza-se-redujeron-casi-a-la-mitad-en-la-ultima-decada-2946445.

Bonilla, M., and Torres, M. (2018). "Enfoque diferencial étnico de la Red de Protección Social contra la Extrema Pobreza en Colombia." *Reflexión Política*, *20*(39), 235–252. https://doi.org/10.29375/01240781.3305.

Departamento Administrativo para la Prosperidad Social (DPS). (2012). "Presidente Santos fue cogestor por un día en Cali" [video]. YouTube, February 29. https://www.youtube.com/watch?v=L5lpnDfKYHs.

Departamento Administrativo para la Prosperidad Social (DPS). (2018). "Legado para la prosperidad." https://dps2018.prosperidadsocial.gov.co/ent/Documentos%20compartidos/Libro_Legado_para_la_Prosperidad-jun2018.pdf.

Departamento Nacional de Planeación (DNP). (2019). "Pobreza monetaria y pobreza multidimensional. Análisis 2008–2018." November. https://colaboracion.dnp.gov.co/CDT/Desarrollo%20Social/Documento%20de%20An%C3%A1lisis%20de%20las%20Cifras%20de%20Pobreza%202018.pdf.

Echeverry, C. (2014). "Acompañamiento familiar de la estrategia Red Unidos para la Superación de la Pobreza Extrema. Experiencias de dos familias del municipio de Dagua, Valle. 2009 a 2013." Universidad del Valle, Documentos de Trabajo—CIDSE 012335.

Econometría Consultores, Institute for Fiscal Studies, Fedesarrollo, & Sistemas Especializados de Información. (2012). "Evaluación de impacto de Unidos—Red de Protección Social para la Superación de la Pobreza Extrema." http://centrodedocumentacion.prosperidadsocial.gov.co/2020/Planeacion/9.Evaluaciones/Subdireccion_Gral_Superacion_dela_Pobreza/2011_UNIDOS_EVALUACIO%CC%81N%20DE%20IMPACTO%20RED%20DE%20PROTECCIO%CC%81N%20SOCIAL%20PARA%20LA%20SUPERACIO%CC%81N%20DE%20LA%20POBREZA%20EXTREMA_37.pdf.

Ley 1785 de 2016. (2016). "Por medio de la cual se establece la Red para la Superación de la Pobreza Extrema—Red Unidos y se dictan otras disposiciones." June 21. https://dapre.presidencia.gov.co/normativa/normativa/LEY%201785%20DEL%2021%20DE%20JUNIO%20DE%202016.pdf.

Ramírez, X. (2012). "Plan de Gobierno y empresarios para erradicar la pobreza." *La República*, February 29. https://www.larepublica.co/responsabilidad-social/plan-de-gobierno-y-empresarios-para-erradicar-la-pobreza-2002965.

Steiner, R., Acosta, P., and Vásquez, T. (2010). "Análisis del informe de estado de familias en la Red Juntos." *Fedesarrollo*, August. https://www.repository.fedesarrollo.org.co/handle/11445/349.

7

Poverty, Conflict, and Peace

Correlation between Poverty and Conflict

One special feature makes Colombia a unique and particularly interesting case: the strategy against poverty was put into practice in the middle of an internal armed conflict and, at the same time, during peace negotiations with the main illegal armed group. This group was nothing less than the oldest and most powerful guerrilla army in Latin America: the Revolutionary Armed Forces of Colombia, known as the FARC, an organization that had been fighting the Colombian State for half a century.

Undoubtedly, poverty and war feed into each other. Therefore, the country's effort to make peace was also an effort for social inclusion that ultimately allowed the State and its social support programs to reach areas of the country that had been isolated for decades.

In February 2020, the World Bank released an in-depth and revealing study titled "Fragility and Conflict: On the Front Lines of the Fight against Poverty," which highlights the close link between these two scourges—poverty and war—and the difficulty of reducing poverty levels in areas where conflict and institutional weakness have reigned (*El Tiempo*, 2020). Regardless of war-affected territories' natural resources, populations in these territories cannot take advantage of them due to violence and uncertainty. Rather, these resources become spoils fought over by armed actors, who often work to serve others with shady interests seeking to profit from the situation.

According to the World Bank study:

> people living in fragile and conflict-affected situations (FCS) are more likely to suffer multiple deprivations than those in other places. One in five suffer from monetary, education, and infrastructure deprivations simultaneously. Economies in FCS lag behind non-FCS economies in all aspects of human capital—people's health, education, and skills. Conflict deaths and institutional fragility are associated with lower economic growth rates.
>
> (World Bank, 2020)

The Battle Against Poverty. Juan Manuel Santos, Oxford University Press. © Juan Manuel Santos (2023).
DOI: 10.1093/oso/9780192885234.003.0008

Countless circumstances in conflict zones threaten human dignity and exacerbate the phenomenon of poverty: families' displacement from their homes and their productive plots of land, young people's recruitment into the war by illegal groups and also by the State, the lack of investment, the destruction of transport and service infrastructure, attacks against populations, the planting of landmines that turn the countryside and roads into deadly traps ... in short, every scenario of desolation and stagnation produced by any armed confrontation.

I remember an anecdote from the early 1990s, when I was the minister of foreign trade, which illustrates very well how war scares off productive investment. Together with the minister of finance, I traveled to New York to participate in a meeting, organized by Chemical Bank, with a group of American chief executive officers (CEOs) interested in the possibility of investing in Colombia. We were in the middle of the meeting when news broke of a terrorist attack in Bogotá, a bomb that had claimed many victims. The meeting, naturally, was not as successful as we had hoped. At the end of the event, the president of one of the participating companies approached me and said something that stuck with me: "As long as you have that war in your country, it's going to be very difficult for you to attract investment. Capital is no friend of war."

A few years later, Nelson Mandela, one of the people I most admire, made a similar comment to me. I had a long conversation with him in Midrand, South Africa, in April 1996, when I traveled there to turn over the presidency of the United Nations Conference on Trade and Development (UNCTAD) to him. At the end of our conversation, Mandela said something to me that echoed the words of that businessman in New York: "Peace is an essential condition for development. If you don't have peace, Colombia will not take off."

It is possible to extrapolate this statement to the issue of poverty: the absence of peace makes it more difficult, almost impossible, to reduce poverty. Why? War creates poverty—it's that simple—and poverty facilitates the emergence and protraction of conflict. Therefore, the two priorities of my administration complemented each other: reaching a peace agreement that would put an end to 50 years of internal armed conflict and substantially lowering poverty rates by significantly improving the quality of life of the most vulnerable Colombians.

I always saw the fight against poverty as a logical and natural complement to peace. Guerrilla groups in Colombia used poverty and social inequality as justification for their existence and their fight against the State. Some call these "objective causes." This justification is very controversial, however, because it is always possible to seek out paths to build equity without having to resort to weapons and violence, which only produce misery. Yet, apart from that, it cannot be ignored that people's poverty and vulnerability are a breeding ground for social unrest and, for some, to make the wrong choice and take up arms. In a prosperous and egalitarian society, there would hardly be guerrilla groups like the ones we Colombians have had to endure.

In other words, poverty does not justify violence, but a tangible improvement in the living conditions of the poorest population is indeed a necessary condition for sustainable and lasting peace. Peace alone is not enough; it must always be accompanied by effective social policy.

There is another relationship between poverty and war, which very few consider. I'd like to explain it using a family anecdote. When my youngest son, Esteban, finished secondary school, he decided to serve in the army, not to begin a career as an officer but as a simple private soldier. His training—during which he had no kind of privileges, even as the president's son—was a school of life for him, just as it had been for me when I was in the navy. Not only did he learn discipline and military skills, but he also interacted with young people from all Colombian regions and from the humblest social classes. I remember him telling me, "Dad, a lot of my fellow soldiers couldn't even eat three times a day at home. This is the first time they have been able to. They come from the poorest of the poor." This experience gave my son a social awareness that he still has, but I bring it up for a reason. This wasn't only the case with army soldiers but also with the young people who joined—voluntarily or by force—the ranks of illegal armed groups. The first victims of war are young people without opportunities who have to fight on one side or the other of a conflict. Battles are always fought by the poorest, not by the most privileged members of society. The poor pay with their lives.[1]

Reparations and Land for Victims and Small-Scale Farmers

In an earlier chapter, I mentioned how Congress approved a legal initiative for compensating victims of the internal armed conflict and returning the land of thousands of small-scale farmers who had been displaced from their plots by violent actors. This initiative, made possible through a coalition of political

[1] This is related to what Professor Amartya Sen narrates in his book *Identity and Violence: The Illusion of Destiny* (Sen, 2007). When Professor Sen was 11 years old, he witnessed the murder of a Muslim man who had arrived in a Hindu neighborhood simply to look for work. This led Professor Sen to write his book's reflection on identity and violence.

forces that supported us in Congress and ensured our ability to govern, was Law 1448 of 2011, known as the Victims and Land Restitution Law. I signed it on June 10, 2011, with Ban Ki-moon, United Nations Secretary General at the time, as a witness.

This law has a very special feature: the State committed to compensating victims before the conflict ended. This means that victims' reparation did not result from a peace process but rather that we wanted to get ahead of the peace negotiations because we understood we couldn't keep postponing a solution for this humanitarian calamity. This was the first time a country began recognizing and providing reparations to victims of an armed conflict on its soil before the conflict had ended. The law entered into force on January 1, 2012, and we didn't reach the peace agreement with the FARC until November 2016. Many asked me why we did it. Why didn't we wait until the peace agreement was signed? I replied to them, "There are more than eight million victims (today, more than nine million registered victims). If we don't start now, we'll never finish."

This law established institutions such as the Victims' Unit, in charge of the process for registration, individual care, and reparation of the victims of the conflict, and the National Center for Historical Memory, which has the mission of compiling documents and testimonies that record the history of the armed conflict in Colombia. Both entities became affiliated with the Department for Social Prosperity when the social inclusion and reconciliation sector was established. The Land Restitution Unit was also established as an entity under the Ministry of Agriculture. This unit was in charge of leading the process to return the property of victims who were dispossessed or displaced by illegal armed actors.

Originally, a ten-year period—between January 2012 and December 2021—was established for fulfilling the Victims and Land Restitution Law's objectives. These notably include providing reparations to the entire universe of victims, who represent, as mentioned, more than 9 million Colombians today, and returning the land, via court ruling, of all those who had lost or abandoned it because of the violence. It was, and still is, an enormous job. Consequently, a new law extended the period by another ten years, so it now expires in December 2031.

Here, I must digress somewhat to explain the impact of a change in political direction on the implementation of this ambitious initiative and many others related to the peace process that culminated in the agreement to end the conflict with the FARC, which we signed in November 2016. Iván Duque, my successor as president, who took office on August 7, 2018, belongs to the Centro Democrático (Democratic Center), a political party led by my predecessor, Álvaro Uribe, who vehemently opposed the negotiation and signing of the peace agreement, even though he himself had tried to start a similar process. From a right-wing perspective, this party preferred to continue seeking a military solution to the conflict rather than negotiating a peace agreement. In other words, it preferred to annihilate the enemy, which would entail another 10 or 20 years of confrontation and the human, social, and economic costs inherent in this, rather than making some concessions to the guerrilla group, as is customary in any peace negotiation.

With the peace agreement's initial phase of implementation just beginning, I handed over power to a president and a party that opposed the agreement. That, of course, led to a slowdown in fulfilling many of the signed commitments and also in executing the Victims and Land Restitution Law. Although this law did not stem from the peace process, former President Uribe and his political group had also opposed it because, among other reasons, it officially recognized the existence of the armed conflict, a necessary condition to be able to negotiate under the protection of the Rome Statute.

Fortunately, Colombia is a country with a strong institutional structure, and a substantial part of the peace agreement was incorporated into the Constitution. Thanks to this, and despite the Duque administration's unwillingness to fulfill certain aspects of the agreement and its hostile actions to torpedo it (e.g. when it objected to fundamental aspects of the law that put the Special Jurisdiction for Peace into practice), commitments with the victims have continued to be fulfilled. However, it must be said, they have progressed at an ostensibly slower pace than that of my administration. I still hope that subsequent administrations will have a much more positive and proactive attitude, which will make it possible to meet the ambitious targets set for the remaining years.

On April 9, 2022, the country commemorated its annual National Day of Memory and Solidarity with Victims, and an assessment was conducted of the progress made in more than ten years of the Victims and Land Restitution Law being in force. At the end of my mandate, in 2018, we had delivered humanitarian assistance and aid to four million victims and economically compensated close to 900,000. According to official figures, in April 2022, there were 9,263,826 people registered as victims. Of these, 1,217,423 have received compensation (Ríos, 2022; Varela, 2022, pp. 153–154). Only an additional 300,000 victims have received compensation in 4 years. This means that the next three administrations, beginning with the recently inaugurated one, must step on the accelerator in order to finally deliver justice to that immense proportion of the Colombian population that has been victimized and that, for the most part, is part of the poorest population in the country.

Another fundamental aspect to consider in the effort to establish peace and reduce poverty is that of land. Land ownership and work on the land have been at the root of all the conflicts Colombia has experienced since its independence, and they are also the cause of terrible economic inequality. While a few landowners own enormous estates, many of which remain unproductive or are used for extensive cattle ranching, a large majority of small-scale farmers subsist with the bare minimum on small plots, in conditions of extreme poverty. Of Colombia's 40 million hectares of productive land, only seven million are used for agricultural activities, while the rest is grazing land for livestock.

To begin the arduous process of small-scale farmers returning to the lands they left due to the armed conflict, we had to establish more than one entity. In addition to the Land Restitution Unit, dedicated to this work, we established an agrarian court system with jurisdiction to study the claims that were filed and hand down rulings that would serve as the basis for restitution. To make a very important clarification, these proceedings reverse the burden of proof to avoid revictimizing the dispossessed farmers by forcing them to prove their dispossession. The parties opposing the victims' claims are those who must prove their ownership or legitimate possession of the land. Simply put, the system gives credence to the victims' word, thus facilitating a positive resolution of their lawsuits.

At the end of my government, in August 2018, after having established the administrative and judicial institutions to make land restitution possible, we had returned, via court rulings, more than 300,000 hectares to dispossessed farmers. Another 700,000 hectares remained in judges' hands, pending a ruling on restitution. By March 2022, more than 6,900 rulings had already been handed down, returning more than 538,000,000 hectares to 10,130 small-scale farmer families and 22 ethnic communities that filed collective lawsuits (Ortiz, 2022). As is the case with victims' compensation, this is a lengthy and complex task. It moved forward very slowly during my successor's term, but we hope it will progress more quickly in the remaining time period of the Victims and Land Restitution Law, in force until the end of 2031.

Yet, it's not just about returning land to small-scale farmers who have been dispossessed of it by violence. The peace agreement signed with the FARC includes agrarian development as its first point. We took into account that the FARC guerrilla army had rural origins and that it had always emphasized claims to the land and obstacles for rural development as the cause of its establishment and armed struggle. As an administration, we took advantage of the opportunity to catch up on the age-old debt the State has with the Colombian countryside, which has been excluded from progress for centuries. This first chapter of the agreement included a stipulation to establish a Land Fund calculated at 3 million hectares, primarily consisting of unoccupied public lands or lands that had been illegally acquired, so that farmers with no land, or insufficient land, could have their own land to work. The parties also agreed on a large-scale rural property titling program for those who do not have a land title. This program's goal is to legalize 7 million hectares.

At the end of my administration, and after establishing the National Land Agency to be in charge of these tasks laid out in the peace agreement, we managed to include 200,000 hectares in the Land Fund and legally titled 1,470,000 hectares (*El Tiempo*, 2018). By March 2022, the Land Fund already included more than 1,900,000 hectares, and an additional 1,147,000 hectares had been legally titled (*Semana*, 2022).

If we add the land returned to date to dispossessed small-scale farmers via court ruling to the land that has been incorporated into the Land Fund and the land that has been titled to rural landowners who did not have a property title, we have more than 35,000 square kilometers—an expanse greater than the size of Belgium or Moldova—significant, but still insufficient, progress.

In sum, we made land tenure an essential part of restoring victims' violated rights and of the negotiations that culminated in the peace agreement with the FARC. Today, there are entities—the Land Restitution Unit, the agrarian courts, the National Land Agency—dedicated exclusively to returning plots of land to dispossessed farmers, to growing a Land Fund for poor farmers that need plots, and to legalizing the property of farmers who own the land but do not have a legal deed. All these actions, implemented in the Colombian countryside, the area most affected by violence and also by poverty, are resulting in better living conditions and, above all, better income-generating opportunities for hundreds of thousands of families in rural Colombia.

The Peace Agreement's First Point and the Multidimensional Poverty Index

In addition to the issue of land, three other aspects related to the Multidimensional Poverty Index (MPI) were agreed in Point 1 of the peace agreement.[2]

---

[2] The recent book by Londoño and Velásquez (2022) provides a comprehensive overview of both progress and challenges in implementing the comprehensive rural reform laid out in the Peace Agreement.

The first is the implementation of the Development Programs with a Territorial Focus (PDETs in Spanish) in 170 municipalities of the country. These municipalities were chosen not only because they had been deeply impacted by violence—including violence by the FARC—and the absence of State services but also because of their impoverished conditions. In 2017, the National Planning Department (DNP in Spanish) found that, according to the 2005 population census, the MPI was 72.8% in PDET municipalities, well above the national average of 49% (DNP, 2017, p. 10). Using the MPI helps to guide the government's priority actions to reduce poverty in the areas most affected by violence in the country. Subsequently, the National Administrative Department of Statistics (DANE in Spanish) released an official multidimensional poverty rate for PDET municipalities, which was published at the end of 2021 and will continue to be regularly published. The report presents an aggregate MPI for PDET municipalities: 34.7% in 2018, 30.6% in 2019, and 32.9% in 2020 (DANE, 2021, p. 28). This tool will allow those who implement the plans and programs established in the Final Agreement's text to monitor progress on implementation in the 170 prioritized municipalities.

Second, another component of Point 1 is the implementation of a series of National Plans for Comprehensive Rural Reform (Final Agreement to End the Armed Conflict and Build a Stable and Lasting Peace, 2016, pp. 24–33). Cognizant that the conflict and poverty have been more intense in rural areas, the peace negotiators agreed on the implementation of 16 national plans covering all rural areas in the country. These plans directly address the C-MPI's five dimensions and 15 indicators. Consequently, they will comprehensively contribute to reducing multidimensional poverty in rural areas. The 16 plans are:

1. Rural housing
2. Tertiary roads
3. Connectivity
4. Electrification
5. Drinking water and basic sanitation
6. Rural health
7. Rural education
8. Marketing
9. Technical assistance
10. Irrigation
11. Income generation

12. Solidarity economy
13. Right to food
14. Social protection
15. Environmental zoning
16. Titling of rural property.

Third, to implement the Final Agreement, the DNP developed a roadmap called the Framework Plan for Implementation. This document "grounds" in practice the targets, indicators, and parties responsible for the different components of implementation. One of the key targets of Final Agreement implementation, according to this document, is to reduce multidimensional poverty by 50% in the country's rural areas by 2031 (Gobierno de Colombia, 2017).

All these aspects illustrate the MPI's importance and relevance to the agreement's implementation and peacebuilding. In fact, Point 1.3, "National Plans for Comprehensive Rural Reform," explicitly states the need to use a multidimensional approach to poverty in rural areas:

The central objective of the national plans for Comprehensive Rural Reform is, on the one hand, to overcome poverty and inequality, in order to achieve the well-being of the rural population, and on the other, the integration of and closing of the gap between rural and urban areas. In accordance with this Agreement, the competent authorities must draw up and start up National Plans in the territory.

Poverty is overcome not simply by improving families' income, but by ensuring that boys and girls, men and women have adequate access to public goods and services. This is the basis of a decent life. Thus, overcoming poverty in the countryside depends, first and foremost, on the joint action of the national plans for Comprehensive Rural Reform, which over a fifteen-year transition phase will eradicate extreme poverty, reduce rural poverty in all its dimensions by 50%, reduce inequality and create a trend towards the convergence, at a higher level, of the quality of life in towns and cities and in the countryside. In any case, the framework plan must guarantee that the utmost efforts are made to fulfil the National Plans in the next 5 years. In order to overcome poverty, specific, differentiated measures will be implemented to address the special needs of women in the countryside and achieve effective equality of opportunity between men and women.

(Final Agreement, 2016, p. 24)

Victims' Example: Encouragement to Persevere

With more than 9 million victims of the internal armed conflict, recognizing and providing reparations to this universe of victims exceeds the efforts of any single administration. Colombia has 50 million inhabitants, so we are talking about 18% of the population. That is why it was so important for us to begin this work in 2012 and for the nation to collectively continue these efforts and fully complete this work by 2031.

When we began reaching out to the FARC about a possible peace agreement during my administration, I thought the victims of the armed conflict were going to be the main opponents. It is well known that every peace process requires making concessions on both sides, and one concession is usually amnesties or reduced sanctions for conflict actors, particularly those belonging to illegal armed groups. I imagined that those who had experienced violence firsthand, who had been displaced from their lands, who had lost loved ones or been injured or maimed, were going to oppose such concessions. Much to my surprise, I found that the vast majority of victims in the country supported the peace process without reservation. They did so for an altruistic reason, which many of them expressed when I met with them: "We support the peace process because we don't want other Colombians to experience what we experienced."

In the first phase of the process, Professor Ronald Heifetz, founder of the Center for Public Leadership at the Kennedy School of Government at Harvard University, where I had studied, came to visit me in Bogotá. He gave me a piece of advice that was extremely helpful. He said:

> Mr. President, you're beginning a journey that is full of obstacles and difficulties. You were elected because, as minister of defense, you demonstrated your success in waging war; now, you have the opportunity to make peace, and you'll find that it's much more difficult. You're going to be discouraged many times, tempted to give up on your purpose. I recommend that, whenever you feel beaten down, hopeless, try speaking with victims of the war rather than speaking with your advisors. Meet the victims and listen to their stories. With their courage and their generosity, they will give your heart strength and your head reasons to persevere.

I must say, I followed his advice to the letter. I asked the director of the Victims' Unit to see to it that I spoke with a victim of the conflict at least once a week. Sometimes, they visited me in my office. At other times, most of the time, I met with them when I was traveling to the country's various regions. When we would meet, I'd ask them about their story and their family's story, about the difficult circumstances they had experienced, about the way in which they were rebuilding their lives, and about their hopes. Each conversation left a mark on my heart. I felt the pain of what they shared with me, but I was much more amazed by their capacity for resilience and their solidarity.

While many people in the country who hadn't experienced the effects of violence criticized the peace process and demanded a relentless form of justice for the guerrilla fighters making peace, which, in practice, meant giving up entirely since no guerrilla fighter signs an agreement to lay down arms only to go to prison, the victims, who did know about the suffering and misery left by war, were absolutely generous. They told me that, more than seeing their perpetrators behind bars, they were mainly interested in knowing the truth about what had happened to their loved ones, many of whom had been disappeared. And, of course, they had expectations about reparations.

They told me numerous stories. Although this is not the time to repeat them all, I believe sharing just one helps to understand the dimension of victims' contribution to peace in Colombia. It is the story of Pastora Mira—a story that made Pope Francis shed tears when he visited Colombia in September 2017. Pastora is a humble woman, originally from a small town in the department of Antioquia, who experienced the nightmare of war in many ways. Her father and her first husband were murdered. She was displaced from her town by guerrilla and paramilitary violence. Paramilitaries disappeared one of her daughters, whose body was only found seven years later. And this illegal armed group also tortured and murdered her youngest son. Three days after his burial, a wounded young man knocked on her door, and she took care of him without asking who he was. When his health improved, the young man saw the photos of her son and confessed, amid sobs and despair, that he was part of the group that had murdered him. He even told her how they had tortured him before killing him.

Pastora, instead of condemning him, hugged him and said, "Thank you for telling me the truth about what happened to my son. And thank you for letting me take care of you and forgive you."

"But why?" this man asked, astonished. "I just told you I tortured and killed your son!"

"Because with what you did, I won't have to live with that hate for the rest of my life," she answered. Today, Pastora is a social leader who devotes her time to supporting the recovery of other people who, like her, have been victims of violence.

When they announced I had won the Nobel Peace Prize, the first thing I thought was that I wanted a delegation of victims to accompany me to receive the medal since we conducted the peace process for them and because of them. The Nobel belonged to them. Pastora and other victims were with me at Oslo City Hall on December 10, 2016 when I was given the prize. At one point in my speech, I asked them to stand up to receive the tribute they deserved. It was very exciting to hear the lengthy applause from the ceremony attendees, beginning with King Harald V of Norway and his family. It was a recognition not only of the victims present but also of those 9 million Colombians—victims of violence, and also of poverty—who overwhelmingly defended peace.

Their hard life stories fueled me to persist in an effort to bring not only peace to my country but also well-being to those who suffered because of the war. For me, it was truly a life lesson.

Territorial Peace: Development for Conflict-Affected Regions

A specific feature of the peace process with the FARC is that it focused on victims and on protecting their rights to truth, justice, reparation, and non-repetition. Beyond ceasing armed confrontation, the final agreement created a series of measures to support and improve the living conditions of those fellow citizens who had lost so much—their loved ones, their land, their health, their personal integrity—because of the violence.

The enormous social gap between urban and rural areas is indisputable. To give an example, in 2020, while the C-MPI stood at 12.5% in municipal seats (meaning municipalities' urban areas), it was 37.1% in rural areas: a difference of 24.6 percentage points (Becerra, 2021).

For this same reason, every effort aimed at ending the armed conflict—which mainly affected the Colombian countryside—must necessarily lead, in the medium and long term, to an improvement in the social conditions of rural areas in the country. In turn, this improvement will contribute to reducing this gap.

In the peace agreement signed on November 24, 2016, the following was included among the general principles for its implementation:

Territorial integration and social inclusion: the measures taken during the implementation must promote the integration of territories within the regions and the integration of the regions within the country, as well as the inclusion of the different populations and communities, in particular those most affected by the conflict and those which have lived in conditions of poverty and marginalization.

(Final Agreement, 2016, p. 205)

This commitment to improve the living conditions of "those most affected by the conflict and those which have lived in conditions of poverty and marginalization" came to life in the establishment of the abovementioned Development Programs with a Territorial Focus (PDETs in Spanish).

What are the PDETs? They are development programs, designed with the active participation of the beneficiary communities, who decide and prioritize works and investments. They are implemented in the areas most affected by the armed conflict, which, as a result of the conflict, have had less State presence and higher poverty rates in the past decades. In other words, they are a mechanism to bring prioritized social investment to the regions hardest hit by the war.

According to the text of the Final Agreement, the PDETs aim:

to achieve the structural transformation of the countryside and the rural environment and to promote an equitable relationship between rural and urban areas, with a view to guaranteeing: [...] Well-being and quality of life for people living in rural areas—boys and girls, men and women—by enabling them to exercise their political, economic, social and cultural rights and reversing the effects of poverty and conflict.

(Final Agreement, 2016, p. 22)

Sixteen PDET areas were identified, including 170 of the country's 1,102 municipalities, with more than 6.6 million residents. Higher poverty rates, greater presence of illicit crops and illegal mining, weak presence of institutions, and greater impacts of the armed conflict were found in these areas, which are now receiving social investments, in consensus with communities, called to transform the lives of millions of Colombians in rural areas.

The economist Mauricio Cárdenas, minister of mines and energy and minister of finance in my administration, summarizes it well:

Many things can be said about the living conditions in these regions, but to put it simply, if they formed a country, it would be the poorest in Latin America, the worst in terms of infrastructure, the most violent, and, intertwined with all this, the country with the highest share of illegal activities in its economy [...]

The negotiators of the peace agreement with the FARC were fully aware of this situation. They prioritized closing the gaps between the Colombia where most of us live and that other Colombia where, in addition to conflict, unlawfulness, and poverty, there is enormous institutional instability. We cannot speak of lasting and sustainable development if we do not first resolve this situation.

(Cárdenas, 2020)

At the end of 2018, the last year of my administration, 13 of the 16 PDETs had been signed, and the others were more than 90% completed. They were all developed with the active participation of local communities. These programs are true territorial roadmaps to combat poverty and improve the quality of life in the prioritized areas, with a 15-year implementation period beginning as of their launch in 2019. Today, all 16 PDETs are signed and operating. Thanks to them—that is, thanks to the peace agreement that established them—today, the most abandoned regions of the country have a much more positive outlook for development and progress.

With an investment of nearly 3.3 billion dollars, 33,000 initiatives developed by local people themselves are beginning to be implemented, including projects for roads, agriculture and livestock, health, education, housing, drinking water, and economic reactivation (Archila, 2022). Where do the resources to finance these projects come from? They are mainly from the country's mining and energy royalties. As a result of a constitutional reform that we proposed to Congress and was approved in 2017, 7% of these royalties are allocated for this purpose.

The PDETs represent bringing together peace agreement implementation, territorial integration, and the fight against poverty in an ideal way; the commissioner for peace in my administration, Sergio Jaramillo, once called this "territorial peace." Today, thanks to the peace agreement's signing, development and progress are being brought to regions that, for decades, were abandoned to their fate, hostage to an absurd conflict that plunged them into misery.[3]

---

[3] Sadly, a cloud of suspicion descended on the management of resources for PDET projects after two renowned investigative journalists, Valeria Santos and Sebastián Nohra, released a public report at the end of June 2022. Apparently, in a corruption scheme that has been taking place since 2019 and that may involve officials from the DNP, control bodies, regional leaders, congressional representatives, and contractors, commissions totaling about 12% of these resources were being charged in exchange for projects being awarded to certain municipalities and contractors. Investigation and control entities and judges are expected to clarify the truth about this very delicate matter, prosecuting and sentencing the responsible parties if this proves to be the case (Santos and Nohra, 2022).

From Coca to Lawfulness

Poverty, State absence, and violence led thousands of families of small-scale farmers in Colombia, beginning in the 1980s, to grow a plant for which mafias and guerrilla groups would pay them more than what they'd receive for any other traditional product: coca. This crop, considered illicit, is the base of the cocaine sold and consumed underground across the world, especially in the most developed nations. In Colombia, it became the main means for subsistence in different areas, mainly those furthest from urban centers, where authorities have little control, such as border areas and forested areas in the Amazon and Orinoquía regions.

Since the Single Convention on Narcotic Drugs was signed at the United Nations in 1961 and United States President Richard Nixon decreed the so-called war on drugs in 1971, a fierce battle has been waged in Colombia against drug trafficking organizations and cartels but also against the farmers who plant coca, who represent the weakest and most vulnerable link in the drug chain.

Half a century later, this war on drugs has proved to be a complete failure. The use of narcotics continues to rise, new drug lords quickly replace the criminals arrested, and small-scale farmers, in the face of limited opportunities, continue to plant coca. Colombia, in particular, has been a victim—as a country, the biggest victim—of this erroneous approach. While we have to devote enormous efforts and budget to combating drug trafficking, thousands of our best men and women—military officers, police officers, judges, journalists, politicians—have died in the spiral of violence and corruption produced by this illegal business.

As long as there is demand, there will be supply. And as long as prohibition continues, there will be incentives for criminals to remain at the forefront of this activity. Many economists warned of this before 1961, and renowned experts repeat it today. Meanwhile, the Colombian State has used all kinds of mechanisms to combat it: crop fumigation, aerial and maritime interdiction, extradition, and military and police pursuit. In the middle of this war, small-scale farmers, as always, bear the brunt of it.

When we began discussing the negotiating agenda with the FARC, I insisted to my delegates at the negotiating table in Havana that the issue of illicit drugs must be part of the agreement. The reason was very simple: the FARC took part in the drug-trafficking business and profited from it. In fact, resources from drug trafficking are what allowed them to sustain themselves for a long time, over and above the resources derived from their kidnappings and extortion. So, just as they had been part of the problem, they now had to become part of the solution.

Ultimately, one of the chapters in the peace agreement was devoted to addressing the issue of illicit drugs with innovative solutions. Up to that point, the State's main weapon against illicit crops had been aerial glyphosate spraying. This pesticide killed not only coca plants but also other legal crops surrounding them. In March 2015, the World Health Organization (WHO) reported that it is probably a carcinogenic substance and harmful to human health. Apart from this, fumigation proved to be highly inefficient.

Small-scale farmers who depended on coca production as their sole source of sustenance replanted it faster than the State could spray or forcefully eradicate, and they also invented all kinds of techniques to prevent the herbicide from affecting the plants. They even covered the leaves of the bushes with raw cane sugar. Aware of this, taking into account the WHO study, as well as an order issued by the Constitutional Court, my administration suspended glyphosate spraying in 2015. We were left with the only alternative of forced manual eradication, which was also very inefficient due to the high percentage of replanting. If small-scale farmers do not have an alternative source of income, they simply replant. Therefore, the best solution was to implement comprehensive programs for voluntary crop substitution that would give farmers profitable and viable alternatives to swap out coca for legal products. According to the United Nations, the replanting rate of voluntarily substituted illicit crops is only 0.4%, compared to a replanting rate of forcibly eradicated crops ranging between 40% and 70% (Díaz, 2020). Based on these figures, the decision was obvious.

What did the peace agreement establish on the issue of illicit drugs? The agreement principally outlined a comprehensive program for eradicating and substituting illicit crops. "Comprehensive" in what sense? Not only would small-scale farmers commit to stop planting and producing coca, but the State would also guarantee them a stable income from legal crops. This resulted in the establishment of the Comprehensive National Program for the Substitution of Crops Used for Illicit Purposes.

In this program, families receive cash assistance for two years while they substitute their crops, and social and livelihood investments are made to ensure the sustainability of their new legal activity. These investments are agreed with communities and families. More than 99,000 coca-growing families joined the program, and over 45,000 hectares were voluntarily eradicated, with less than 1% replanted.

Unfortunately, my successor's administration, keener on using force than reaching social agreements, did not support the program for voluntary substitution of illicit crops that resulted from the peace agreement. Rather, it wasted its four years in office on insisting, especially with its policy of repression and prohibition, on forced eradication and resuming the use of glyphosate spraying. Ultimately, it did not succeed in this due to the environmental and public health requirements laid down by the Constitutional Court. The hard-line approach failed yet again, and Colombia ended up with more than 200,000 hectares of coca and an upsurge in cocaine production stemming from an increase in productivity. As I have said so many times: the war on drugs has only strengthened organized crime and, after all these efforts and costs, we are not better off. It is like pedaling a stationary bicycle.

I must insist that until the international community gains awareness and builds sufficient consensus about the absurdity of continuing a war on drugs based on repression and prohibition and about the need to assess more effective methods, such as regulation or legalization, the voluntary eradication of illicit crops, together with economic support and livelihood projects for small-scale farmers who stop planting coca, is the best social solution to the root problem of drug trafficking. Supporting small-scale farmers in isolated areas of the country to abandon illegal crops for a productive legal activity is another way of not only combating poverty but also cutting off fuel for violence.

A New Outlook of Building Together

Upon signing the peace agreement with the FARC in November 2016, 13,000 guerrilla fighters, including militia members making up their urban support network, began the reincorporation process, placing confidence in a new life of lawfulness. Since then, more than 95% have continued this process and have kept their word not to return to violence, despite the fact that more than 300 former FARC members have been assassinated since the agreement's signing. In the face of this situation, my successor's administration showed neither sufficient strength nor determination to solve this delicate problem, which has rightly dismayed the international community.

Amid this uncertainty, ex-combatants have been building a new life, thanks to the economic and livelihood support outlined in the agreement. Some have chosen to follow their own individual path, but many have partnered with each other—and even with former members of paramilitary groups, their greatest enemies, or with victims of the conflict—to develop livelihood projects of all kinds and seek a way to sustain their families. These range from agriculture, livestock, and agribusiness projects to commercial or handicraft manufacturing enterprises.

In my particular case, at the Compaz Foundation, which I established with resources from the Nobel Prize to support and empower victims of the conflict and to contribute to peacebuilding and reconciliation, we have seen the capacity and talent of thousands of people who now pursue various projects. These include projects such as honey, cocoa, or organic coffee production; the cultivation and processing of peach palm (*chontaduro*, a fruit that only grows in some countries of Latin America), sugar cane, or various Amazonian fruits; the production of products woven with the fiber of the fique plant; craft beer manufacturing; and even the provision of tourist services in areas that previously could not be visited because of the war.

Colombia is still not at total peace. After the demobilization and disarmament of most of the FARC's leaders and members, a small percentage of dissidents from this guerrilla group continued to commit crimes, as did the National Liberation Army (ELN)—a more geographically concentrated guerrilla group with far fewer members, with whom we had begun a peace process that my successor's administration later aborted—and criminal gangs involved in drug trafficking. However, despite these disturbing factors still present today, the peace agreement led to a considerable reduction in violence in most of the country and opened the possibility for Colombians to return to regions that had previously been closed due to conditions of insecurity.

No peace process is perfect, and neither was ours. Nevertheless, over 13,000 men and women handed over nearly 9,000 individual weapons, more than 500 collective weapons to support combat, more than 38 tons of explosives, and over 11,000 hand grenades, among other materials that produce pain and death. Steering these former combatants away from the path of arms signified a giant step forward for Colombia and its future.

It was also—and this is why I mention it in this book—a step forward for the fight against poverty in the country. As long as there is war, it will be very difficult to reach the most vulnerable people in society with social programs, especially because there are territories practically excluded from State actions. As long as there is war, budget resources will primarily have to be allocated to sustaining and equipping the armed forces instead of to education, health, housing, and social infrastructure. As long as there is war, young people—wearing the uniform of legitimate State forces or the uniform of irregular forces—will be cannon fodder, not people building the country.

When I witness—through the projects we support at Compaz Foundation—the joint effort of Colombians who, just a few years ago, were killing each other in the country's forests and mountains, to work and prosper through innovative enterprises, I confirm that signing the peace agreement was also a tool to plant the seeds of coexistence and to strengthen the only war that is worth waging: the war against poverty.

Lesson 7
Peace and Social Development Go Hand in Hand

If war produces poverty, and poverty is a breeding ground for war, it seems obvious that any peace process that attempts to end an armed conflict should establish measures or commitments aimed not only at ending the conflict but also at alleviating and improving the social conditions that motivated it or helped perpetuate it. However, historically, this has not been the case—neither in Colombia nor in the world.

The overwhelming majority of peace agreements focus on establishing steps for the cessation of hostilities and the fate of combatants who decide to return to lawfulness; that is, they focus on what peace process jargon calls DDR: the disarmament, demobilization, and reintegration into civilian life of ex-combatants.

But peace is much more than the silence of guns. If we do not attack the roots of the disagreements and injustices that have given rise to the conflict; if we do not protect victims' rights to truth, justice, reparation, and non-repetition; if we do not take the opportunity to build dignified and equitable social conditions at all levels of society, we are planting the seeds of a new conflict.

We understood this in Colombia. Consequently, the peace process we conducted with the FARC is today considered a model of innovation and comprehensiveness for the world; beyond discussing conditions for DDR, the process placed the victims and their rights at the center of the discussion. Furthermore, it sought to propose solutions and measures to improve the population's living conditions, especially in the countryside. I am sure that the full implementation of the peace agreement with the FARC will solve many of the problems that the country currently faces.

One of the most important institutions worldwide in the study of conflicts and peace processes, the Kroc Institute for International Peace Studies at the University of Notre Dame, affirmed that "Colombia's Final Peace Agreement is more comprehensive than any other agreement signed since 1989" (Kroc

Institute for International Peace Studies, 2020). John Paul Lederach, a professor of international peacebuilding at this institute, said, "Comparatively, the Colombian accord offers one of the most promising platforms to ensure sustainable peace" (Lederach, 2016).

This concept—sustainable peace—is very important. Reaching an agreement on ex-combatants' laying down of arms and reintegration can provide a time of peace, but if peace is to be truly sustainable and lasting, a peace agreement must include aspects that have been, in some way, the "root causes" and also the consequences of a conflict: land tenure and productivity, the recognition and rights of victims, a solution to the illicit drugs problem, women's rights (gender equality), and ethnic communities' rights, all within a human rights approach.

That was what we did when we succeeded in reaching an agreement—against the stubborn opposition of those who preferred a solution using force—to end the conflict with the strongest and oldest guerrilla army in Latin America: in the agreement, we included social aspects that would help Colombia to be a more just and equitable country after making peace.

As Mandela told me, "Peace is an essential condition for development." Today, I am certain that peace and social development must go hand in hand. That was the principle that inspired us in the Havana negotiations. As a result, the Colombian peace agreement can serve, and should serve, as an example and model to many nations that are still simultaneously experiencing the scourges of war and poverty.

References

Archila, E. (2022). "Construcción de paz, con norte y ejecutorias." *El Tiempo*, April 10. https://www.eltiempo.com/opinion/columnistas/emilio-archila-penalosa/construccion-de-paz-con-norte-y-ejecutorias-columna-de-emilio-archila-664451.

Becerra, L. L. (2021). "Pobreza multidimensional golpeó 3 veces más al campo colombiano." *Portafolio*, September 3. https://www.portafolio.co/economia/finanzas/pobreza-multidimensional-hogares-del-campo-los-mas-golpeados-de-colombia-555859.

Cárdenas, M. (2020). "Covid-19 y posconflicto." *El Tiempo*, June 26. https://www.eltiempo.com/opinion/columnistas/mauricio-cardenas-santamaria/covid-19-y-posconflicto-columna-de-mauricio-cardenas-511740.

DANE (National Administrative Department of Statistics). (2021). "Pobreza multidimensional—Agregado municipios PDET" [PowerPoint slides],

December 29. https://www.dane.gov.co/files/investigaciones/condiciones_vida/pobreza/2020/presentacion-ext-pobreza-multidimensional-IPM-PDET-20.pdf.

Díaz, E. (2020). "Resiembra de narcocultivos con sustitución voluntaria es 0,4%." *El Nuevo Siglo*, February 15. https://www.elnuevosiglo.com.co/articulos/02-2020-resiembra-de-narcocultivos-con-sustitucion-voluntaria-es-04.

DNP (National Planning Department). (2017). "Caracterización: Territorios con Programas de Desarrollo con Enfoque Territorial—PDET" [PowerPoint slides], July. https://colaboracion.dnp.gov.co/CDT/Poltica%20de%20Vctimas/Construcci%C3%B3n%20de%20Paz/Caracterizaci%C3%B3n%20PDET.pdf.

Echavarría Álvarez, J., Gómez Vásquez, M., Forero Linares, B., Ramírez Rincón, A., Rodríguez Contreras, A. M., Serrano Idrovo, C., Sáez Florez, C., Ditta, E., Gutiérrez Pulido, E., Martin, G., Zúñiga García, I., Márquez Díaz, J., Quinn, J., Joshi, M., Balen Giancola, M., Cabanzo Valencia, M., Restrepo Ortiz, N., McQuestion, P., and Menjura Roldán, T. (2022). "Cinco años después de la firma del Acuerdo Final: Reflexiones desde el monitoreo a la implementación." Kroc Institute for International Peace Studies/Keough School of Global Affairs. https://doi.org/10.7274/z029p270x6d.

El Tiempo. (2018). "Fondo de Tierras tiene 200.000 de 3 millones de hectáreas previstas." March 1. https://www.eltiempo.com/politica/proceso-de-paz/fondo-de-tierras-tiene-200-000-de-las-3-millones-de-ha-previstas-188892.

El Tiempo. (2020). "Desafío de reducir pobreza, en jaque, según el Banco Mundial." February 27. https://www.eltiempo.com/economia/sectores/reducir-la-pobreza-extrema-mas-dificil-en-zonas-de-conflicto-banco-mundial-467118.

Final Agreement to End the Armed Conflict and Build a Stable and Lasting Peace. (2016). November 24. https://www.peaceagreements.org/viewmasterdocument/1845.

Gobierno de Colombia. (2017). "Plan Marco de Implementación. Acuerdo final para la terminación del conflicto y la construcción de una paz estable y duradera." https://colaboracion.dnp.gov.co/CDT/Conpes/Econ%C3%B3micos/3932_Anexo%20B_Plan%20Marco%20de%20Implementaci%C3%B3n%20(PMI).pdf.

Kroc Institute for International Peace Studies. (2020). "Tres años después de la firma del Acuerdo Final de Colombia: Hacia la transformación territorial. Diciembre 2018 a noviembre 2019." University of Notre Dame. http://peaceaccords.nd.edu/wp-content/uploads/2020/06/Cuarto-Informe-Final-with-Annex-Link.pdf.

Lederach, J. (1997). *Building peace: Sustainable reconciliation in divided societies*. United States Institute of Peace Press.

Lederach, J. P. (2016). "Colombia's Peace Agreement." *New York Times*, November 25. https://www.nytimes.com/2016/11/25/opinion/colombias-peace-agreement.html.

Londoño, R., and Velásquez, M. (eds). (2022). *La reforma rural integral. Debates, acuerdos y trasfondo histórico.* Universidad de Los Andes, Escuela de Gobierno Alberto Lleras Camargo, Ediciones Uniandes.

Ortiz, M. I. (2022). "En los últimos 10 años se han restituido 538.212 hectáreas a víctimas." *El Tiempo.* March 29. https://www.eltiempo.com/justicia/servicios/restitucion-de-tierras-balance-de-entregas-a-victimas-del-conflicto-a-2022-661522.

Ríos, J. (2022). "Las deudas que siguen pendientes con las víctimas del conflicto." *El Tiempo*, April 10. https://www.eltiempo.com/justicia/paz-y-derechos-humanos/victimas-del-conflicto-lenta-reparacion-a-afectados-por-la-guerra-664274.

Santos, V., and Nohra, S. (2022). "Los recursos de la paz: así se direccionaron los proyectos del Ocad Paz." *Blu Radio*, June 29. https://www.bluradio.com/nacion/los-recursos-de-la-paz-asi-se-direccionaron-los-proyectos-del-ocad-paz-pr30.

Semana. (2022). "Así se administran los predios de la Nación." *Semana*, March 5. https://www.semana.com/hablan-las-marcas/articulo/asi-se-administran-los-predios-de-la-nacion/202200.

Sen, A. (2007). *Identity and violence: The illusion of destiny.* Penguin Books India.

Varela, M. (coordinator). (2022). "No enreden la paz. Balance multipartidista de la implementación del Acuerdo de Paz a julio 2022." Congreso de la República, July. https://883ff833-f600-42c2-9780-e8c06ea212bb.usrfiles.com/ugd/883ff8_ad0af9d45a184baa8a31e8bbc1b6c6db.pdf.

World Bank. (2020). "Fragility and conflict: On the front lines of the fight against poverty." February 27. https://www.worldbank.org/en/topic/poverty/publication/fragility-conflict-on-the-front-lines-fight-against-poverty.

8

The Sustainable Development Goals and the Multidimensional Nature of Poverty

The Sustainable Development Goals

September 25, 2015 was a remarkable day for humanity. On that date, in the main assembly hall of the United Nations in New York, in a special session with the presence of Secretary General Ban Ki-moon and many heads of state from around the world, the General Assembly unanimously adopted—without a single abstention—the 2030 Agenda for Sustainable Development. It would be the roadmap to follow in the next 15 years to meet the challenge of sustainable global development. That year, the world's largest multilateral body was celebrating seven decades since its establishment, and adopting this agenda became its great legacy for the future.

The 2030 Agenda consists of 17 goals called the Sustainable Development Goals (SDGs), encompassing 169 economic, social, and environmental targets. In a way, these goals replace the Millennium Development Goals (MDGs). The MDGs, established in 2000 to be fulfilled by 2015, primarily aimed at reducing poverty and encouraging the development of lower-income countries through aid and cooperation from higher-income countries.

In several respects, the SDGs represent a step forward from the MDGs' original formulation. First, while maintaining an emphasis on poverty reduction, they focus on sustainability (i.e. they introduce an environmental factor), indicating that improving national indicators isn't enough and that the entire model must be made sustainable. The SDGs focus on building equity and thus go beyond monetary poverty indices to address other indicators that more comprehensively reflect people's living conditions.

Second, while in the MDGs the main targets on poverty reduction were based only on income, the SDGs also included multidimensional poverty, which reflects the trajectory that countries such as Colombia have followed over the past decade. In this spirit, the SDGs' formulation set out

The Battle Against Poverty. Juan Manuel Santos, Oxford University Press.
© Juan Manuel Santos (2023). DOI: 10.1093/oso/9780192885234.003.0009

to "end poverty in all its forms everywhere." Including both monetary and multidimensional poverty in the global development agenda constitutes an important step for the fight against poverty.

Third, while the MDGs focused on achieving targets in developing countries, the SDGs set targets for all countries without exception, understanding that problems are interconnected and that solutions must be implemented across all latitudes of the planet. For the first time, these goals engage all United Nations Member States, which must incorporate them in their plans and strategies. Each country faces unique and specific challenges, and so each must set its own national targets within the framework of the SDGs.

On the central issue of poverty, the resolution adopting the 2030 Agenda lays out the following:

> We resolve, between now and 2030, to end poverty and hunger everywhere; to combat inequalities within and among countries; to build peaceful, just and inclusive societies; to protect human rights and promote gender equality and the empowerment of women and girls; and to ensure the lasting protection of the planet and its natural resources. We resolve also to create conditions for sustainable, inclusive and sustained economic growth, shared prosperity and decent work for all, taking into account different levels of national development and capacities.
>
> (United Nations General Assembly, 2015, p. 3)

Notably, all 17 SDGs—not just the first one, which expressly mentions poverty—have to do, in one way or another, with the development of a global strategy against poverty and for sustainable development. The SDGs are:

1. No Poverty
2. Zero Hunger
3. Good Health and Well-Being
4. Quality Education
5. Gender Equality
6. Clean Water and Sanitation
7. Affordable and Clean Energy
8. Decent Work and Economic Growth
9. Industry, Innovation, and Infrastructure
10. Reduced Inequalities
11. Sustainable Cities and Communities
12. Responsible Consumption and Production

13. Climate Action
14. Life below Water
15. Life on Land
16. Peace, Justice, and Strong Institutions
17. Partnerships for the Goals.

Few people know, even in my country, that Colombia played a leading role in the initiative to create the SDGs. We proposed this idea at the Rio+20 summit in 2012, and on September 25, 2015, it became none other than the global agenda for the next 15 years.[1]

For that reason, I was invited to speak at that historic inaugural session of the United Nations Summit on Sustainable Development. In my speech, I celebrated this progress for humanity and summarized some of Colombia's achievements on poverty and inequality:

> My country celebrates and welcomes these goals as we are aware they are also necessary conditions for building peace. In turn, peace in Colombia will have very high dividends, precisely in economic, social, and environmental terms. It will be a virtuous circle.
>
> In the next 15 years, together, all countries of the world must meet our three greatest challenges: eradicating poverty in all its dimensions, combating inequality and injustice, and tackling climate change.
>
> The Millennium Development Goals guided us toward a more equal present. In my country, we saw significant progress that was reflected in a better quality of life for the most vulnerable Colombians.
>
> Today, for the first time in Colombia, there are more people in the middle class than people living in poverty.
>
> Income poverty decreased by about 12 percentage points in the last five years, meaning there are 4.4 million fewer Colombians in this condition. This makes us the country in Latin America that has most reduced poverty in recent years. Something similar happened with extreme poverty, with more than 2.5 million people rising out of it.
>
> And a very important accomplishment: we made progress on reducing inequality. Of course, there's still a long, long way to go. Therefore, our challenge now is to boost and make this progress irreversible.
>
> (Santos, 2015)

---

[1] The book by Caballero and Londoño (2022) gives an in-depth perspective of the negotiations and phases that led to the global agreement on the SDGs.

An Initiative by Colombia for the World

Colombia's active participation in bringing the SDGs to life is a story that deserves to be told. It shows how, through meticulous work and effective multilateral diplomacy, it is possible for a country, without being a global power, to help unite the world around a new development paradigm.

The story begins in January 2011. Paula Caballero, a historian and expert in international relations who served as the director of environmental, economic, and social affairs at Colombia's Ministry of Foreign Affairs, was the first to suggest the idea of replacing the MDGs with the SDGs. She told Minister María Ángela Holguín about this project, who welcomed it and entrusted her deputy minister, Patti Londoño, to team up with Caballero and carry the idea forward. Caballero had worked for many years with the United Nations Development Programme (UNDP) in Latin America, helping to develop projects for submission to the Global Environment Facility. In addition, at the Ministry, she had taken part in negotiations on the Aichi Biodiversity Targets and in other negotiations related to climate change. All of this helped her to develop the idea of proposing global goals that kept the focus on poverty, but within a broader concept of sustainability, and that involved all countries worldwide, not just developing countries.

Foreign Minister Holguín, Deputy Minister Londoño, and Director Caballero met with me at the Casa de Nariño, and they suggested the undeniably novel idea of replacing the MDGs with much more ambitious goals that would involve developed countries and include an important environmental component. I remember Paula bruised my ego when she said, "Mr. President, this is your opportunity to lead something actually significant at the global level." Her proposal's relevance, timeliness, and comprehensive nature convinced me, and I gave it my full support.

The process wasn't easy. When word began to get out about the initiative, some accused Colombia of wanting to end the MDGs early since it was 2011 and these goals lasted until 2015. Fortunately, Guatemala and Peru joined the proposal, and little by little, the idea began to take shape. All of this required time and patience. At the United Nations, issues of climate change, development, and biodiversity have independent bodies and discussion forums, and our SDG proposal included all of them. There were several consultations and meetings in Colombia and New York to gain support from other countries. Deputy Minister Londoño and Director Caballero traveled across the world explaining and promoting the initiative, until a consensus was reached on this issue.

As president, my role was to support them politically. With that intent, I devoted myself to promoting the matter with all heads of state with whom I met, as did Minister Holguín with her respective counterparts. In countless meetings that I had with leaders from other countries between January 2011 and September 2015, I told them about the SDGs and their advantages, and I asked them for their support.

Worth highlighting is a very timely conversation I had in Bogotá with UN Secretary General Ban Ki-moon when he came to witness the signing of the Victims and Land Restitution Law in June 2011. Ban, with whom I'd developed a good friendship—in fact, we still work together today as part of The Elders group—was already on the same wavelength about replacing the MDGs with something more ambitious.

I also discussed the matter with Pope Francis when I visited him at the Vatican to request his support for our peace process. I must say, it didn't take much effort to convince him: no one was more interested than the pope in promoting greater social justice in the world and defending the environment. He has addressed these issues in his encyclicals—especially in *Laudato Si'*, but also somewhat in *Fratelli Tutti*. He always supported the SDGs enthusiastically. And here is a curious fact: the first person to mention the SDG initiative to the pope was my ambassador to the United Nations, Néstor Osorio. Osorio, whom I had instructed to promote the SDGs, had been elected president of the UN Economic and Social Council, and he went to visit His Holiness to update him on the world's economic and social situation. The subject came up, and the pope was hooked.

Multilateral diplomacy is not an easy matter. From my first job, as a very young man, when I was a representative of Colombia to the International Coffee Organization in London in the 1970s, I learned the patience and tact, empathy, and level-headedness necessary to move any initiative forward. Later, in the 1990s, as minister of foreign trade, I participated in the negotiations to transform the General Agreement on Tariffs and Trade into the World Trade Organization. It was also my responsibility to preside over the eighth session of the United Nations Conference on Trade and Development (UNCTAD), which advocates so much for countries in the Global South, a position I turned over to Nelson Mandela a few years later.

Life has given me the opportunity to participate in many multilateral negotiations, and that is precisely why I am a strong defender of multilateralism. It is very unfortunate that some—such as President Trump during his time—have disdained and wanted to weaken it. That is a serious mistake. The COVID-19 pandemic has reminded us that no one is alone in this world. If we want to survive and move forward, for example, with tackling the existential challenge of climate change, we must recognize our interdependence and the need to work together. Instead of weakening it, strengthening multilateralism is imperative.

Amid the complexity of multilateral diplomacy, it is notable that we succeeded in moving the idea for the SDGs forward and that the international community unanimously adopted these goals.

In my view, this is the most important thing the United Nations has done in this century. It represents a great example of what can be achieved when there is political will. This achievement was reflected, initially, in the decision to create the concept of the SDGs and a structure to define them. This decision was made at the United Nations Conference on Sustainable Development held in Rio de Janeiro in June 2012 (better known as Rio+20). I personally went to formulate and stand up for the proposal.

In paragraph 246, this conference's final document, titled "The Future We Want," expressly establishes:

> We recognize that the development of goals could also be useful for pursuing focused and coherent action on sustainable development. We further recognize the importance and utility of a set of sustainable development goals, based on Agenda 21 and the Johannesburg Plan of Implementation, which fully respect all the Rio Principles, taking into account different national circumstances, capacities and priorities, are consistent with international law, build upon commitments already made, and contribute to the full implementation of the outcomes of all major summits in the economic, social and environmental fields, including the present outcome document. The goals should address and incorporate in a balanced way all three dimensions of sustainable development and their interlinkages. They should be coherent with and integrated into the United Nations development agenda beyond 2015, thus contributing to the achievement of sustainable development and serving as a driver for implementation and mainstreaming of sustainable development in the United Nations system as a whole. The development of these goals should not divert focus or effort from the achievement of the Millennium Development Goals.
>
> (United Nations, 2012)

The same document resolved (in paragraph 248) "to establish an inclusive and transparent intergovernmental process on sustainable development goals that is open to all stakeholders, with a view to developing global sustainable development goals to be agreed by the General Assembly." It also set out the establishment of an open working group, comprised of 30 representatives nominated by Member States, to develop and submit a report to the United Nations General Assembly with a proposal for sustainable development. Colombia was part of this group, sharing its seat with Guatemala.

After Rio, the UN Secretary General established another body to work in parallel, which he named the High-Level Panel of Eminent Persons to Advise on Planning the Post-2015 Agenda (International Institute for Sustainable Development, 2012). Its mission was to feed good ideas to the open working group and to clean up the different proposals. The group had 26 participants from all over the world, including famous people such as Paul Polman, former chief executive officer (CEO) of Unilever and a great environmentalist, and even a touch of royalty with Queen Rania of Jordan. Colombia's foreign minister, María Ángela Holguín, also took part, always joined and advised by Paula Caballero, who never stopped promoting and nurturing the initiative she had devised. In this group, Colombia insisted on making sustainability a cross-cutting issue. This initially produced resistance, but it was later accepted and today is a core element of the SDGs.

The work of these two groups produced 12 goals, which later increased to 17. The goals were formally approved as the new global agenda at the historic UN General Assembly session on September 25, 2015, presided over by Mogens Lykketoft, who was also the speaker of the Danish Parliament. The entire world, literally, represented in the General Assembly Hall, celebrated with joy and applause when the resolution was adopted without a single objection or abstention. I felt immense joy because the nations of the globe had been able to agree, with Colombia's help, to work for a better, more peaceful, fairer, more sustainable future, with concrete and measurable targets.[2]

Colombian Strategy for SDG Implementation

Due to the SDGs' significance and global effect, their approval by the United Nations General Assembly represented a very high point for Colombian diplomacy. But this international accomplishment was not enough; we had to make them a reality in our country.

Upon my return from New York, I told my Cabinet that I wanted Colombia not only to be the first to make the SDGs into a national law but also to be the first to regionally localize them. This meant bringing the SDGs

---

[2] The complete story of the SDGs' creation and the part Colombian diplomacy played in this process can be read in Caballero and Londoño (2022).

to every department so they could incorporate them into their respective development plans and take ownership.

Thanks to several ministers' work, coordinated by the National Planning Department (DNP in Spanish), we succeeded. At the same time, the SDGs had just been defined within the United Nations and in Colombia we were approving the National Development Plan for my second term of government, 2014–2018. This allowed us to align—in real time—our national agenda with the global development agenda. And we were the first country to do so.

We designed our 2014–2018 National Development Plan—which we titled "Todos por un nuevo país" ("All for a New Country")—and which included three strategic core areas that made up a virtuous circle: peace, equity, and education—with the vision of achieving the SDGs. This was a first step toward the irreversible eradication of poverty and toward a kind of development that improves human conditions and preserves the environment. And I say "a first step" because we sought for this agenda to be fulfilled and implemented not only by my administration but also by future administrations, until we steered into the destination port in 2030.

On June 9, 2015, I signed Law 1753, which issued the National Development Plan. Three-and-a-half months later, the SDGs were officially adopted by the UN General Assembly as the new global agenda. As a result of our involvement from the beginning in the SDGs' origins and definition, we were able to anticipate them at the national level to make them part of our roadmap toward the future.

To make the long-term planning vision entailed in the SDGs a reality, we established in Colombia, as of February 2015, the High-Level Interinstitutional Commission for the Preparation and Effective Implementation of the Post-2015 Development Agenda and Its Sustainable Development Goals, also known as the SDG Commission. Members of this commission include the Office of the President, represented by a high-level presidential advisor; the ministers of finance, foreign affairs, environment and sustainable development, and science, technology, and innovation; and the directors of the DNP, National Administrative Department of Statistics (DANE in Spanish), and Department for Social Prosperity (DPS in Spanish). The director of the Presidential Agency for International Cooperation of Colombia and a private-sector leader joined them as permanent guests. This commission aims to coordinate the SDGs' implementation in the country, in addition to designing methodologies for cross-sectoral work and for evaluation, measurement, and monitoring. We were clear from the beginning that, if we wanted to make the right decisions, we had to have reliable data and indicators that show us where we're at, how we're moving forward, and where we're lagging behind.

Additionally, on March 15, 2018, the National Council for Economic and Social Policy (CONPES in Spanish) approved CONPES Document No. 3918, which includes the strategy for SDG implementation in Colombia. This document laid out something very important, part of the SDGs' guiding principle to "leave no one behind": it is not enough for Colombia, as a country, to fulfill the SDGs, but each and every one of its regions must also fulfill them, without a single one lagging behind. With this in mind, the document decided "to specify the territorial scope for the SDGs' fulfillment using the regional localization of the indicators and set targets with the purpose of closing the existing gaps and achieving higher levels of well-being in the country" (CONPES, 2018, p. 35).

Regional targets were set based on the unique characteristics of each region.[3] These serve as a guide for policy actions in the territories. To define them, national targets were used as a starting point and then adapted to the regions. Thanks to this, in Colombia, the SDGs are a frame of reference and constitute a port of destination not only at the national level but also at the territorial level, given that they include indicators for each of the country's regions.

In this way, Colombia was a pioneer not only for having proposed the establishment of the SDGs in 2011 and having reached a global commitment to work on them at the Rio+20 Conference in 2012 but also because it included them in its National Development Plan even before they were adopted by the world and because it has established a comprehensive strategy for their implementation, measurement, and monitoring at both national and regional levels.

When United Nations Secretary General Ban Ki-moon came to Cartagena in September 2016 to accompany the signing of the peace agreement with the Revolutionary Armed Forces of Colombia (FARC), I remember him warmly congratulating us for this historic breakthrough for reconciliation but also for our role in the SDGs' design and implementation. He said that these two achievements made Colombia a true global example. Later, in the General Assembly itself, he remarked that we had become the best news in the very complex world he had to deal with.

---

[3] Six regions in the country were defined: (1) the Caribbean region, (2) the Central-South-Amazon region, (3) the Central-Eastern and Bogotá region, (4) the coffee region and Antioquia, (5) the Llanos region, and (6) the Pacific region.

Use of the C-MPI to Measure Progress on the SDGs

The annex "Global Indicator Framework for the Sustainable Development Goals and Targets of the 2030 Agenda for Sustainable Development" establishes concrete targets for each country to meet for each SDG. Under Goal 1 (End poverty in all its forms everywhere), Target 1.2 outlines the following commitment:

> By 2030, reduce at least by half the proportion of men, women and children of all ages living in poverty in all its dimensions according to national definitions.
>
> (United Nations, 2015)

If reducing the proportion of people living in poverty "in all its dimensions" by at least half is the aim, it is obvious that the most appropriate indicator to monitor this target is the Multidimensional Poverty Index (MPI). This is understandable because the only way to lift a person or a family group out of poverty is to ensure that their basic needs, in all dimensions of their lives, are properly met. It is not enough to improve one condition or another if other conditions continue to fall short.

Therefore, various countries, including Colombia, decided to adopt the MPI as an official indicator to monitor the first SDG, related to poverty eradication. In the process of preparing CONPES Document No. 3918 of 2018, which set the strategy to implement the SDGs in Colombia, a series of workshops were held. Public officials from 44 national government entities participated in them. As an outcome, these workshops identified the country's indicators and defined its 2018 and 2030 targets. In total, 156 indicators were designed, each with a leading institution responsible for its management. These indicators would enable measuring the country's progress on the 17 SDGs.

Of course, monitoring 156 indicators is a complex task. Therefore, Colombia decided to focus its attention on what the CONPES document called "16 major national government commitments to fulfill the SDGs," each represented by "16 established indicators, which will be specifically monitored and will have a plan for following up on financing for the fulfillment of the SDGs" (CONPES, 2018, p. 33).

It is not surprising that the indicator defined to monitor the first SDG, No Poverty, is the Colombian Multidimensional Poverty Index (C-MPI). According to the CONPES document, the multidimensional poverty baseline in 2015 was 20.2%, the national target for 2018 was to lower this index to 17.8%, and the ambitious national target for 2030 is to bring it down to

8.4%.[4] In 2016, we met the 2018 target ahead of schedule, with a C-MPI of 17.8%. Unfortunately, this index increased by 2018 and reached 19.6% (1.8 percentage points above the target).[5]

In 2021, the National Administrative Department of Statistics (DANE in Spanish) reported a C-MPI of 16%.[6] This suggests that the C-MPI must practically be cut in half in the remaining nine years of the 2020s if the national target established for 2030 is to be met. On average, this requires a decrease of about 0.85 percentage points per year. The goal remains achievable, but it will require a sustained and determined effort by the two administrations that will lead Colombia between 2022 and 2030 to attain good economic growth that is complemented by effective social policies and programs, such as the ones already discussed that we launched in the previous decade.

For now, for the purposes of this book, it should be noted that the C-MPI, which we adopted in a pioneering way in 2011, has become the main indicator to define our country's progress on the first SDG. Two important Colombian initiatives—the creation of the SDGs and the official adoption of the C-MPI as an instrument for monitoring and targeting social policy—have come together to make our progress on the 2030 Agenda more effective and surefooted. Indeed, this agenda is humanity's most comprehensive and ambitious commitment to ensuring a sustainable future for the world's men, women, and children, as well as the planet itself. Today, after the COVID-19 pandemic, this commitment has taken on even greater importance and relevance.[7]

Climate Change and Poverty

I cannot conclude this chapter on the SDGs and their relationship with poverty without mentioning, even briefly, the tremendous challenge of climate change. This is not just any challenge but an existential one—meaning that the survival of our species depends on it.

Two unique events related to climate change took place at the beginning of my administration, in August 2010. The first was my visit to the representatives of four Indigenous peoples—the Kogui, Arhuaco, Wiwa, and Kankuamo peoples—in the Sierra Nevada de Santa Marta, an impressive mountain

[4] Percentages calculated using projections based on the 2005 census. If the updated methodology with the 2018 census projections were used, the 2015 baseline would be 19.8%.
[5] For comparability, percentages calculated using projections based on the 2005 census.
[6] Percentage calculated using projections based on the 2018 census.
[7] A complete analysis on using the MPI to monitor the SDGs in Colombia can be found in Zavaleta and Moreno (2018).

formation in northern Colombia near the Caribbean Sea. On August 7, the day I took office as president, I wanted to make a symbolic gesture of respect for the original inhabitants of our territory. Early that morning, I traveled to the Sierra Nevada to visit them, speak with them, and ask for their permission to be sworn in by Congress that afternoon.

I met with the *mamos*—that is, the leaders of those four peoples, who call themselves our "older siblings." They explained their world view to me, a world view in which respect for nature plays an essential role. The *mamos*, in an act of trust, gave me a traditional wooden baton and said:

> This baton we give you is a symbol of power, which you must use for the good of all. In particular, we hope that you will achieve two very important things. First, achieve peace. Without it, we can't live with peace of mind in our territories. We have suffered deeply from the internal conflict. Many of our brothers and sisters have died or have had to abandon their land, and we need peace more than anything else. But we also ask you to make another kind of peace: peace with Mother Nature. She is angry because of the way we treat her, the harm we do to her, and she's going to react to that harm. You, as a government leader, will have to suffer the consequences of this reaction. That's why it's so important for you to make peace with her. Nature is our life, it's everyone's life: ours, as your older siblings, and yours, as our younger siblings.

On that same occasion, in addition to the baton, they gave me a necklace with four stones. They told me, "One represents land, which we must take care of; another represents water, which is the source of life; another represents nature, which we must be in harmony with; and the fourth represents government, which must respect the order of nature and the Creator's will."

This experience with the *mamos* transformed my life. I had already been cultivating an awareness of ecological responsibility, but this conversation made me reaffirm it with conviction and purpose: to do everything possible to protect natural resources and the environment in my country and in the world.

Hardly a week after my inauguration, the *mamos*'s prophecy was fulfilled. The worst phenomenon of La Niña hit our country with full force, causing floods and disasters throughout our territory. I had to deal with the problems of a flooded nation for practically the first two years of my administration. This forced me to lead an aggressive environmental policy, resulting in important progress that has been recognized by the international community. I remember inviting Al Gore, the former United States vice-president and a Nobel Peace Prize laureate for his environmental work, to Colombia.

In a long conversation, Gore gave me an unforgettable lesson about the threat of climate change and about our vulnerability, the consequences of which we were experiencing firsthand.

My predecessor had not placed much emphasis on environmental issues, to the point that he had eliminated the Ministry of the Environment and had merged it—using reasoning difficult to decipher—with the Ministry of Housing. One of my first steps was to reverse this merger and to re-establish the Ministry of Environment and Sustainable Development. Of course, the most urgent matter was assisting the hundreds of thousands of people affected by the harsh rains. We launched a program called Colombia Humanitaria (Humanitarian Colombia) in which official entities and the private sector came together to lend a helping hand to families who had lost their homes, animals, and belongings. And we went further, taking advantage of the distressing situation to create a comprehensive set of institutions to prevent and respond to natural disasters, led by a new entity called the National Unit for Disaster Risk Management. Today, we have a risk prevention and response system that is perhaps the most comprehensive and efficient in Latin America.

It is important to ask: when a natural disaster occurs, who usually suffers the most? The answer is simple: the poor. When rivers overflow or when there are droughts, when the ground quakes, when rain washes away homes in the mountains, the poor are those most affected. Therefore, a policy of preventing and responding to the risks associated with natural disasters is also a way of combating poverty.

Per square kilometer, Colombia is the most biodiverse country in the world. This means it has enormous privilege and many opportunities to take advantage of this natural wealth. However, at the same time, due to its geographical position between two oceans and its mixed terrain of mountain ranges, plains, and forests, our country is highly vulnerable to the effects of climate change. This dual condition—of being a biodiverse and vulnerable country like few others—has made us especially active in supporting initiatives to curb global warming and greenhouse gas emissions. In my administration, we demonstrated that commitment in many ways.

During the 8 years of my administration, we succeeded in protecting— hopefully permanently—43 million hectares of forests and natural areas, more than 20% of our continental and marine territory. This equates to a protected area larger than Germany or Japan.

To give just one concrete example, we more than tripled the Chiribiquete Natural National Park in our Amazon region, which the United Nations Educational, Scientific and Cultural Organization (UNESCO) declared to be both a natural and cultural world heritage site. Today, Chiribiquete is one of the largest natural parks in the world—much larger than Serengeti, in Africa—and is also one of the parks that concentrates the greatest biodiversity and the most unexplored rock paintings.

The *páramos* (a kind of alpine tundra ecosystem) are a particularly important ecosystem for the environment as they are natural water factories. Half of the world's *páramos* are concentrated in Colombia, and another task we carried out was to delimit and protect all of the country's *páramos* (37 in total) from activities that could damage them, such as mining.

We also promoted moderation, so necessary for preserving humankind's limited resources. We created the first carbon tax in Latin America and a tax on plastic bag use. We met the Aichi target on protection of coastal and marine areas ahead of schedule. And we proactively supported the Paris Agreement adopted at the United Nations Climate Change Conference (COP 21) in December 2015.

With all these actions, among various others, we wanted to leave a legacy of responsibility to future generations not only in Colombia but also in the entire world. And we also aimed for poor families, the most vulnerable in every sense, to have a lower risk of experiencing the consequences of what—I repeat—is the greatest existential threat to humanity: climate change.

Lesson 8
Everything Is Interconnected

In my inaugural address, which I delivered in the Plaza de Bolívar in Bogotá on August 7, 2010, I quoted a phrase from a wise naturalist: "We don't inherit the Earth from our ancestors, we borrow it from our children." This phrase expresses the extent of our responsibility to the planet and to future generations. We are not the Earth's owners but its tenants. And as tenants, if we want to live well and make progress equitably, we must take care of what Pope Francis has called "our common home."

In 2018, when I went back to the Sierra Nevada de Santa Marta to return the traditional baton and the ceremonial necklace that the *mamos* had given me, as well as to bid them farewell as president, they surprised me by saying I could keep them because my work wasn't finished. In our conversation, they warned me that the SDGs' social, economic, and environmental dimensions were very good but that they lacked a fourth dimension that is, perhaps, the most important one: the spiritual dimension.

The spiritual dimension, they explained to me, refers to the intrinsic, vital, essential connection between humans and nature. It refers to that dialogue that must exist between our soul and the spirit—the vibration, the energy—of plants, animals, and even minerals. We must align ourselves with that spirit if we want to survive as a species. It refers to the ethical rules of respect, moderation, and balance that our "older siblings" have tried to teach us and that they have practiced for millennia.

Nothing can be taken from nature without first asking for permission and giving something in return. When we break this rule, we begin walking toward the edge of a cliff. The proof of this is climate change.

When we speak of the SDGs, we are speaking of vital commitments that concern all the world's nations, whether developed or developing, without exception. We must reduce poverty and inequality in our countries, that is clear, but we must do it within a context of environmental sustainability so that social progress is continuous and translates into a real improvement in living conditions.

In December 2018, in New York, I had the honor, along with Joe Biden, of receiving the Global Visionary Award from Conservation International. I ended my acceptance speech with a few words that sum up an inescapable lesson, which goes beyond any political standpoint or any ideology: the future of the planet and of humanity are inextricably linked, for better or for worse.

> Let's listen, with humility, to the voice of the wise guardians of the earth.
>
> Let's use our limited and invaluable resources in moderation.
>
> Let's understand, with a spiritual approach, that the earth is our mother, and that every tree, every river, every flower, every rock, every air particle are also our siblings.
>
> (Santos, 2018)

References

Alkire, S. (2015). *Multidimensional poverty measurement and analysis* (1st edn). Oxford University Press.

Alkire, S., and Sumner, A. (2013). "Multidimensional poverty and the post-2015 MDGs." Oxford Poverty and Human Development Initiative (OPHI). https://ophi.org.uk/multidimensional-poverty-and-the-post-2015-mdgs.

Caballero, P., and Londoño, P. (2022). *Redefining development: The extraordinary genesis of the Sustainable Development Goals.* Lynne Rienner Publishers.

CONPES, and Departamento Nacional de Planeación (DNP). (2018). "Estrategia para la implementación de los Objetivos de Desarrollo Sostenible (ODS) en Colombia. Documento Conpes 3918." March 15. https://colaboracion.dnp.gov.co/CDT/Conpes/Econ%C3%B3micos/3918.pdf.

International Institute for Sustainable Development. (2012). "UN Secretary-General announces High-Level Panel on Post-2015 Agenda." August 2. http://sdg.iisd.org/news/un-secretary-general-announces-high-level-panel-on-post-2015-agenda.

Oxford Poverty and Human Development Initiative, and United Nations Development Programme. (2020). "Global MPI 2020—Charting pathways out of multidimensional poverty: Achieving the SDGs." https://ophi.org.uk/global-mpi-report-2020.

Oxford Poverty and Human Development Initiative, and United Nations Development Programme. (2021). "Global MPI 2021. Unmasking disparities by ethnicity, caste and gender." https://ophi.org.uk/global-mpi-report-2021.

Santos, J. M. (2015). "Palabras del Presidente de la República Juan Manuel Santos en la Cumbre de Desarrollo Sostenible de Naciones Unidas" [speech transcript]. Misión Permanente de Colombia ante la ONU en Nueva York, September 25. https://nuevayork-onu.mision.gov.co/newsroom/news/palabras-del-presidente-la-republica-juan-manuel-santos-la-cumbre-desarrollo.

Santos, J. M. (2018). "El mundo debe ir más allá de los compromisos de París." El Tiempo, December 8. https://www.eltiempo.com/vida/medio-ambiente/el-mundo-debe-ir-mas-alla-de-los-compromisos-de-paris-302810.

United Nations. (2012). "The future we want." https://www.un.org/disabilities/documents/rio20_outcome_document_complete.pdf.

United Nations. (2015). "Global indicator framework for the Sustainable Development Goals and targets of the 2030 Agenda for Sustainable Development." https://unstats.un.org/sdgs/indicators/Global%20Indicator%20Framework_A.RES.71.313%20Annex.pdf.

United Nations Development Programme, and Oxford Poverty and Human Development Initiative. (2019). "How to build a national multidimensional poverty index (MPI): Using the MPI to inform the SDGs." https://ophi.org.uk/how-to-build-2019.

United Nations General Assembly. (2015). "Resolution adopted by the General Assembly on 25 September 2015. Transforming our world: The 2030 Agenda for Sustainable Development." October 21. https://www.un.org/en/development/desa/population/migration/generalassembly/docs/globalcompact/A_RES_70_1_E.pdf.

Zavaleta, D., and Moreno, C. (2018). "Monitoring SDGs through an MPI: The case of Colombia." Dimensions, November 2. https://mppn.org/sdgs-colombia.

9

Encouraging Results

The Decade That Transformed Colombia

Poverty and Inequality Reduction

By the end of the second decade of the twenty-first century, Colombia had established itself as a success story and a leader in its region. It had reduced both multidimensional and income poverty, resulting in the expansion and consolidation of the middle class. It also showed significant progress in reducing inequality. According to the Economic Commission for Latin America and the Caribbean (ECLAC), "Considering the latest years (2014 and 2017) in the 13 countries where comparable figures are available for the period, only in three (Colombia, El Salvador and Paraguay) did the levels of income inequality decrease" (ECLAC, 2019, p. 44).

We have already cited some of these data points throughout this book, but this closing chapter will summarize them again to give the reader an accurate and quantifiable idea about the concrete results of implementing the described social policies and programs and of adopting the Colombian Multidimensional Poverty Index (C-MPI) as an index that, in addition to measuring multidimensional poverty, helped us to more effectively target State efforts to reduce poverty and improve equity in all respects.

Regarding monetary or income poverty, we lowered the poverty rate from 42% in 2008 to 27% in 2018—a decrease of 15 percentage points in one decade. In addition, regarding extreme monetary poverty, we lowered the percentage of people in this subcategory from 16.4% in 2008 to 7.2% in 2018, meaning that extreme poverty fell by more than 9 percentage points, cut by over half. These percentages are obtained using the Mission for the Splicing of Employment, Poverty, and Inequality Series (MESEP) methodology, which is the only one that enables comparison of the indicated years.[1]

Moving from cold figures to the real data, human beings made of flesh and blood, the situation is summarized in the fact that the total number of people

[1] See the section "An Important Clarification on Changes in the Measurement of Monetary and Multidimensional Poverty in Colombia" at the beginning of this book.

The Battle Against Poverty. Juan Manuel Santos, Oxford University Press. © Juan Manuel Santos (2023). DOI: 10.1093/oso/9780192885234.003.0010

considered to be living in monetary poverty decreased roughly from about 18.5 million in 2008 to 13 million in 2018.[2] Five-and-a-half million people rising above the monetary poverty line is equivalent to the entire population of Finland or the Central African Republic doing so.

Now, let's turn to the results in multidimensional poverty. The first available data corresponds to calculations for 2010. While multidimensional poverty was 29.7% in that year, it had declined to 19.1% by 2018, representing more than a ten-percentage-point decrease.[3]

It is not surprising that the case of Colombia has attracted the attention of analysts and multilateral organizations since the decreases seen—a 15-percentage-point drop in monetary poverty in 10 years and a 10.6-percentage-point drop in multidimensional poverty in 8 years—are not easy for any nation to achieve, much less a country like Colombia, sliced open by an internal armed conflict for so many years.

Thus far, we have focused on the issue of poverty. However, we can't ignore the fact that poverty reduction is of little use if not coupled with a similar trend in inequality, meaning a narrowing of the gap between those who have more and those who have less.

It is well known that the subcontinent of Latin America is currently, and has been for many years, the most unequal region in the entire world. While an absurdly high share of national wealth is concentrated among a few families, the majority of families live in precarious conditions. This produces social unrest, which people often seek to resolve by turning to populist governments, whose "magical" formulas without an economic foundation end up making things worse.

When I became president of my country in 2010, Colombia held the shameful position of being the second-most unequal country, only surpassed by Haiti, in Latin America and the Caribbean—already the most unequal region in the world. We had to pull ourselves out of this situation. In this sense, all the social policies on early childhood care, education, health, housing, access to basic utilities, job creation, and other areas were aimed at producing results not only in reducing poverty but also in closing the enormous social gap.

The coefficient devised by the Italian statistician Corrado Gini, called the Gini index or coefficient, is the measure typically used to assess income

[2] Once again, according to the percentages calculated with the MESEP methodology.
[3] Here, we are using the percentages based on the updated projections with the 2018 census figures.

inequality in a country. The Gini index ranges from 0—the measure of perfect equality, where everyone receives the same income—to 1—maximal inequality, where a single person has all the income and everyone else has none. Therefore, the lower the coefficient, the lower the inequality. Any decrease in this index, however small, represents an enormous step toward greater social equality.

According to the World Bank, the Gini coefficient for Colombia was 0.546 in 2010. After continuously declining, it dropped below 0.5 for the first time in 2017, reaching 0.497. Since then, it has unfortunately risen again, reaching 0.542 in 2020, very close to the level at the beginning of the 2010s (World Bank, 2022). For several years, specifically, between 2012 and 2018, we stopped being at the bottom of the list in Latin America and moved up to an intermediate ranking, a positive trend that began in 2010.

In May 2013, economist Mauricio Santa María, the director of the National Planning Department at the time, explained it as follows:

> ECLAC considers Colombia to be among the countries that have reduced inequality the most in recent years. Why was it reduced? Due to a fundamental event that had not occurred in the last 20 years: the income growth of the poorest people was six times higher than that of the richest people (13.2% vs. 2.3%). In other words, the income that has grown in recent years has been that of the poorest people. This, indeed, is equity. We finally managed to break the growing trend of inequality and, for the first time since comparable figures are available, the economy is growing, the poorest people's incomes are growing, and inequality is diminishing. This trend moves in the opposite direction of the pre-2010 trend, when the economy grew but so did inequality.
>
> (Santa María, 2013)

The Gini coefficient data published by the National Administrative Department of Statistics (DANE in Spanish) is slightly different than the World Bank data since the DANE data is based on the 2012–2021 Great Integrated Household Survey (GEIH in Spanish), while the multilateral body includes other factors. However, it confirms a decreasing trend in the Gini index between 2010 and 2017 (declining from 0.560 to 0.508) and the resumption of an increasing trend between 2018 and 2020, when the index reached a value of 0.544, a regrettable setback.[4] In 2021, the index fell again until it reached 0.523, similar to its 2015 value (DANE, 2022, p. 4). Unfortunately, this decrease does not appear to be structural, given that it is largely

---

[4] See, for 2010, the DANE, ECH, cited in Santos (2020, pp. 359–360).

due to government-delivered assistance to the poorest families during the COVID-19 pandemic. Such emergency assistance is not sustainable over time.

One factor that has historically contributed to reducing, or at least not worsening, inequality has been that in all the years of the twenty-first century (the 22 years between 2000 and today), the increase in the legal minimum wage, the floor above which all workers in the country must be paid, has been higher than the increase in the cost of living; that is, there has been a sustained increase in the real wages—wages minus inflation—of a large majority of workers who earn the legal minimum or a little more (*Portafolio*, 2021).

Another very important indicator for measuring progress on social equality is the growth and strength of the middle class. In Colombia, according to the latest reports, six in ten citizens belong to the middle class, and just under four in ten are poor in terms of income.[5] However, there are two subclassifications within the middle class: some people are in the emerging middle class, which still faces some risk of falling back into poverty, and others are in the established middle class, with higher incomes and less risk.

In 2014, for the first time since this began to be measured, the established middle class surpassed the population living in poverty. This remained the case at least until 2019, before the emergence of the COVID-19 pandemic caused catastrophic social effects.[6] Not only were there more people in the middle class than people in poverty, but there were also more stable and confirmed members of the middle class than people in poverty. As developed countries know and have demonstrated, a strong middle class, with higher incomes and greater capacity for consumption, is a guarantee of progress, development, and social peace.

Of course, much attention must be paid to the percentage of people in the emerging middle class, that is, in that new middle class that feels vulnerable and at risk of falling back into the trap of poverty. This emerging middle class is the one that goes out to protest the most and, in fact, is the one that led enormous social mobilizations in 2019 and 2021, which put the administration at that time in check. The new members of the middle class want guarantees of a better future, of better job opportunities and education. Above all, they don't want pandemics or misguided economic policies to make them lose ground.

---

[5] Taking into account the monetary poverty percentages calculated by the DANE with the methodology updated in 2020.

[6] See the DANE, GEIH, cited in Santos (2020, pp. 60–61, 355).

Progress on Other Social Indicators

We have said that poverty is a multidimensional phenomenon. Keeping this in mind, if Colombia significantly reduced both monetary and multi-dimensional poverty during the 2010s, this reduction must be the product of equally significant improvements in the various dimensions that make up individuals and families' quality of life. I am referring to aspects such as health, nutrition, education, access to basic public utilities, connectivity, and housing.

In the two four-year terms when I was president of Colombia, between 2010 and 2018, we made very important progress in all these areas, but it would be unfair to pretend that these years were an isolated and non-representative period. In general, the various administrations that have governed the country have maintained sound economic and social policies that—some to a greater extent, others to a lesser extent—have contributed to improving Colombians' living conditions.

In August 2020, Editorial Planeta Colombiana published my book *Un mensaje optimista para un mundo en crisis* (*An Optimistic Message for a World in Crisis*). In it, drawing upon verifiable data and statistics, I propose that Colombia can show itself to the world as a success story in terms of its economic and social progress during the three decades between 1991 and 2019. We went from being practically a failed state to a country with some of the best economic and social indicators in the region. During my administration, we became members of the Organisation for Economic Co-operation and Development (OECD).

I know it is always easier and more tempting to see the glass half empty (the persistent shortcomings, endemic poverty, major inequality) than the glass half full (the concrete progress in almost all areas of human life), but I wanted to review this period because, looking back, Colombian society has made surprising progress. I was inspired by the work of Steven Pinker, a professor of psychology at Harvard University, who wrote the foreword to my book. He has demonstrated, with eloquence and unquestionable numbers, that humanity, despite the persistence of conflicts, injustices, and deprivations, continues on a track of advancing and improving its existential conditions.

Professor Pinker himself stated the following in his foreword:

All these victories and setbacks are evident in one of my favorite countries, Colombia, which I have had the privilege of visiting for about 45 years. During that time, life expectancy has risen from 64.5 to 77.1 years. The percentage of the population living in extreme poverty has fallen from 20% to around 7%, with illiteracy plunging almost equally. And although Colombia has seen a tragic increase in the number of homicides, the peak reached in 1991 has fallen to its 1976 level.

(Pinker, 2020)

I wanted to replicate the exercise Pinker had done for the world in a much more targeted setting: Colombia in the last three decades of its history. The results were striking.

✓ GDP per capita, expressed in dollars based on purchasing power par-ity, increased from US$7,465 in 1990 to US$13,332 in 2018—a 78% increase![7]

✓ Inflation—which is, in fact, the worst "tax" on the poor, as they suffer the most from an increase in the cost of living—went from 32.4% in 1990 to 3.2% in 2018.[8]

✓ The unemployment rate, which stood at 10.5% of the economically active population in 1990 and had risen to 20.2% in 2000, fell to 9.7% in 2018. In fact, between 2013 and 2018, for six consecutive years, we kept the unemployment rate in the single digits, something that hadn't happened since 1995.[9]

✓ The quantitative housing deficit, meaning the percentage of households without adequate housing, declined from 17% in 1993 to 5% in 2018.[10]

✓ Public utilities' coverage has grown impressively over the past three decades. Household electricity coverage increased from 77% in 1993 to 97.7% in 2018, and the percentage of households with water services increased from 71% to 86.9% in the same period. Households covered by natural gas utilities rose from 35.3% in 2003 to 64.4% in 2018.[11]

✓ In the twenty-first century, an internet connection is an essential utility. In 2010, only 280 municipalities—out of Colombia's total 1,102—had access to fiber-optic backbone networks, and there were 2.8 million internet connections. By 2018, all municipalities in the country were connected to fiber-optic internet, and there were about 28 million broad-band connections. While only 5.5% of households had internet access in 2003, 52.7% had this service in their homes in 2018.[12]

✓ In terms of education, the budget for this sector tripled between 1998 and 2018 and, as of 2015 and for the first time in history, it became the

---

[7] See World Bank, International Comparison Program database, cited in Santos (2020, pp. 86–87, 357).
[8] See DANE, IPC, cited in Santos (2020, pp. 90–91, 358).
[9] See DANE, 1990–2000 ENH and 2001–2019 GEIH, cited in Santos (2020, pp. 94–95, 358).
[10] See DANE, 1993 and 2018 censuses, cited in Santos (2020, pp. 132–133, 363).
[11] See DANE, 1993 NBI and 2003–2018 ECV, cited in Santos (2020, pp. 136–137, 363).
[12] See DANE, 2003–2018 ECV, cited in Santos (2020, pp. 138–139, 363).

most-funded sector within the national budget. The school dropout rate fell from 7.6% in 1997 to 3% in 2018, and the percentage of young people aged 17–21 who received some kind of higher education (technical, technological, or professional) increased from 15.3% in 1996 to 52% in 2018.[13]

✓ The number of children in comprehensive early childhood education programs rose from 151,312 in 2011 to 1,467,492 in 2018.[14] This was one of the most rewarding achievements for me, given its positive social impact.

✓ Health coverage increased dramatically. While only 29.2% of the population had some kind of health insurance in 1995, 95.2% of Colombians were covered in 2019.[15]

✓ The maternal mortality rate fell from 104.9 deaths per 100,000 live births in 2000 to 45.3 in 2018.[16]

✓ The infant mortality rate dropped from 15.9 deaths of children under one year of age per 1,000 live births in 2005 to 11.3 in 2018.[17]

✓ Finally, among many other advances, Colombia's ranking improved on the Human Development Index, developed by the United Nations Development Programme (UNDP). This index evaluates three basic dimensions: a long and healthy life, access to knowledge, and a decent standard of living. While Colombia ranked 163rd out of 189 countries in 2007, it rose to 79th out of the same number of countries in 2018, placing it in the top half.[18]

All this progress in various areas that add up to Colombians' quality of life attests to a sustained effort by various administrations, civil society, and international cooperation to turn Colombia into a success story of social development.

It cannot be ignored, however, and this is worth emphasizing, that our country continues to lag far behind in almost all indicators compared to the most developed nations in the world. Additionally, in the 2018–2022 period, several of these achievements suffered setbacks due to the disastrous combination of the COVID-19 pandemic and erratic social policy.

[13] See Ministry of National Education, cited in Santos (2020, pp. 146–147, 152–153, 156–157, 364–366).
[14] See Single System of Information on Children (SUIN in Spanish), cited in Santos (2020, pp. 148–149, 364).
[15] See Ministry of Health and Social Protection, cited in Santos (2020, pp. 184–185, 366–367).
[16] See Ministry of Health and Social Protection, cited in Santos (2020, pp. 186–187, 367).
[17] See Ministry of Health and Social Protection, cited in Santos (2020, pp. 188–189, 367).
[18] See UNDP, Human Development Report, cited in Santos (2020, pp. 266–267, 373).

We are a middle-income country that faces complex challenges, such as drug trafficking and remaining violence from some illegal armed groups, with a large territory that social, judicial, and State protection services do not properly reach. We still have a long way to go.

A Policy of Social Inclusion

There are other types of social progress that have less data or statistical monitoring but which are paramount for the just and equitable development of a society. I am referring to progress on inclusion.

A society cannot be considered developed as long as discriminatory or exclusionary behaviors persist for any reason, that is, as long as there are citizens of a lower class than others. Democracy, understood as majority-chosen government, cannot be true democracy unless that government protects and guarantees minorities' fundamental rights. I am convinced of that, and we made progress in that direction—toward the inclusion and protection of minorities—in the two terms of my administration.

A fundamental achievement was Law 1482 of 2011, which seeks to guarantee the protection of individuals or groups of people whose rights are violated by acts of racism or discrimination. This law added a full chapter to the Penal Code, and it included crimes related to acts of racism or discrimination on the grounds of race, ethnicity, religion, nationality, political or philosophical ideology, sex, or sexual orientation. In Colombia today, anyone who prevents, obstructs, or restricts a person from exercising their rights or who incites these acts, for any of the aforementioned grounds, may be subject to sanctions ranging from fines to imprisonment.

Among the wide range of laws that we promoted or supported to improve conditions for minorities are the law for people with disabilities, the law for victims of sexual violence, and the law on feminicide, in addition to advances in public policies on participation and land titling with Afro-Colombian and Indigenous communities.

Working conditions were also improved for domestic workers, community mothers (women who take care of their neighbors' children so that their neighbors can work), volunteers, members of the Colombian Civil Defense (volunteers especially trained to help in cases of natural disasters and other situations that require community actions in solidarity), firefighters, resident physicians who are trained in different specialties, and even the unemployed, through the Law on the Protection of the Unemployed.

This is not to mention the greatest commitment to reparation that a State has ever taken on with its own population: the Victims and Land Restitution Law, which we discussed at greater length in Chapters 3 and 7 of this book.

Perhaps it was Mother Teresa of Calcutta who said, "A society that does not privilege the weakest is doomed to chaos." That is undoubtedly true. Consequently, working against discrimination and racism, against all kinds of exclusion or limitation of people's rights, is a moral and human obligation. Doing so combats the poverty produced by violence and lack of solidarity.

A Valuable Analysis

Has progress been made in the fight against poverty? Was it worthwhile to adopt the Multidimensional Poverty Index in 2011 as an instrument for measuring and also targeting social policies? Did all the programs and policies adopted in the 2010–2018 period serve the greater aim of reaching equality? I believe that this book so far has shown us that the answer is "Yes." In addition, all these actions, properly analyzed and tailored to each case's particular circumstances, can be replicated in many other nations to effectively improve the population's living conditions.

To conclude this chapter and this book, it seems pertinent to quote a newspaper column published in *El Espectador* at the beginning of 2018 and signed by José Manuel Restrepo, who, at the time, was a dean at one of the most traditional and prestigious universities in Colombia: the Universidad del Rosario. Restrepo, with a master's degree in economics from the London School of Economics and a doctorate from the University of Bath, writes a particularly relevant analysis because, after his time as dean, he was a minister during my successor's four-year term: first as minister of commerce, industry, and tourism and later as minister of finance and public credit. This means that Restrepo was in charge of managing the finances and budget of an administration that has not been particularly prone to recognizing the progress made during my administration.

His column, "El real y futuro estado de la pobreza" ("The Real and Future State of Poverty"), written during his time in academia, summarizes very well Colombia's transformation during the past decade, which makes our achievements in the fight against poverty a model likely to be analyzed and studied worldwide:

It is impossible not to recognize the progress that the country has made in reducing poverty. Between 2010 and 2016, poverty has dropped by almost 25%, and if we go back to 2002, there is a 44% drop. Even with the temporary effects of the increase in oil prices on GDP [gross domestic product] and even considering any changes in the methodology to measure monetary poverty, it is foolish to under-value the fact that today, 4.3 million Colombians have risen out of misery. Even extreme poverty has fallen in the same period by almost 70%, pulling an additional 2.3 million citizens out of marginalization.

To counter those who insist on discrediting this progress as a result, they say, of a particular economic model, it is well worth reminding them that this improve-ment also occurs in multiple dimensions. There are improvements not only in the income of families rising out of poverty but also in quality of life, which includes issues related to nutrition, infant mortality, years of schooling, and access to public utilities, among others. This multidimensional poverty indicator shows a decrease of 71% in the same period, 2010–2016, with particular improvements of more than 94% in urban seats in that period.

It is also fair to recall that the Gini coefficient, which measures inequality, was 0.571 in 2002 in Colombia but had improved to 0.517 by 2016. This suggests a 10% decrease in inequality, a step forward that, although it is small (even though Colombia is the country that has made the most progress between 2010 and 2015 in Latin America) and expresses a greater challenge in the future, also refutes the argument of those who insist on the glass half empty of the problem of income distribution.

All of this has enabled consequent achievements such as the reduction of unem-ployment, the construction of a much larger middle class, a decrease in informal unemployment, and the fact that in seven out of the last eight years the increases in the minimum wage have been greater than the sum of inflation and productiv-ity. Having said this, in equity and poverty, the watchword is to never give in or back down and to always try to accelerate.

(Restrepo, 2018)

Lesson 9
Coordinated and Targeted Work Yields Results

As I look back, four years after finishing my term at the helm of Colombia's journey, I see a horizon of dreams, objectives, struggles, challenges, disap-pointments, and results. Most especially, I see what we were able to do—amid the difficulties and criticism every government faces—in two areas that were at the core of my administration: peace and social progress.

The signing of the agreement to end the conflict with the Revolutionary Armed Forces of Colombia (FARC) guerrilla army was a milestone in Colom-bian history as the country began to turn the page on an internal war that had lasted for over half a century and left hundreds of thousands dead and millions of victims and displaced people. For this accomplishment, I was awarded the Nobel Peace Prize. I received the prize aware that it wasn't for me but for the victims of the armed conflict and for our nation, which had signed its hope for a better future in that agreement.

Progress on the issue of equity—in other words, progress on reducing poverty and inequality and improving Colombians' living conditions—has been less visible and, consequently, less recognized. However, it represents a milestone as great as signing the peace agreement or proposing the Sustainable Development Goals because it transformed the lives of millions of fellow citizens for the better, citizens who escaped the poverty trap and progressed toward a life of achievements and rights that were previously unknown to them.

How was this accomplished? In this book, we have aimed to describe this process, which includes, very importantly, the official adoption of the Multidimensional Poverty Index developed and promoted by the Oxford Poverty and Human Development Initiative (OPHI) at the University of Oxford, according to the Alkire–Foster method. Since 2011, the C-MPI has become an essential element of evaluating, analyzing, and guiding public policies, to the point that we incorporated it into national development plans, discussions at the Poverty Roundtable, and the Sustainable Development Goal indicators.

What this book demonstrates, in short, is that coordinated and targeted work yields results, and this was the case between 2010 and 2018 in the fight against poverty. Institutional coordination, enabled through the social inclusion and reconciliation sector's establishment, the Poverty Roundtable and dashboards, the strengthening of Red Unidos, and the continuous leadership of the country's president (a factor that shouldn't be overlooked since political will is the muscle of any government-produced transformation) can produce extraordinary results. May this lesson, which summarizes the previous ones, serve as a guide and inspiration for so many nations on the planet that, like Colombia, continue to fight for more just, equitable, and reconciled societies.

References

DANE (National Administrative Department of Statistics). (2022). "Pobreza y desigualdad. Información pobreza monetaria nacional 2021. Actualizada el 26 de abril de 2022. Comunicado de prensa." April 26. https://www.dane.gov.co/index.php/estadisticas-por-tema/pobreza-y-condiciones-de-vida/pobreza-monetaria.

ECLAC (Economic Commission for Latin America and the Caribbean). (2019). "Social panorama of Latin America 2018." https://www.cepal.org/en/publications/44396-social-panorama-latin-america-2018.

Pinker, S. (2020). "Cómo puede hablarse de progreso en un universo hostil?" [foreword]. In J. M. Santos, *Un mensaje optimista para un mundo en crisis*. Editorial Planeta Colombiana, 12–17.

Portafolio. (2021). "Así ha sido el incremento real del mínimo en los últimos años." December 13. https://www.portafolio.co/economia/asi-ha-sido-el-incremento-real-del-minimo-en-los-ultimos-anos-559571.

Restrepo, J. M. (2018). "El real y futuro estado de la pobreza." El Espectador, January 27. https://www.elespectador.com/opinion/columnistas/jose-manuel-restrepo/el-real-y-futuro-estado-de-la-pobreza-column-735714.

Santa María, M. (2013). "Reducción de la pobreza y la desigualdad." El Tiempo, May 4. https://www.eltiempo.com/archivo/documento/CMS-12779386.

Santos, J. M. (2020). *Un mensaje optimista para un mundo en crisis*. Editorial Planeta Colombiana.

World Bank. (2022). "Gini index—Colombia. 1992–2020." https://data.worldbank.org/indicator/SI.POV.GINI?locations=CO%26most_recent_value_desc=false.

Epilogue

The Process Continues

In August 2018, when I completed my second term in office, the poverty statistics showed a significant decrease.

According to the Mission for the Splicing of Employment, Poverty, and Inequality Series (MESEP) methodology (the one used by the National Administrative Department of Statistics (DANE in Spanish) between 2010 and 2019), monetary poverty had fallen from 40.3% in 2009 to 27% in 2018, and extreme monetary poverty had been halved from 14.4% in 2009 to 7.2% in 2018.

If the methodology updated in 2020 based on the recommendations of the Committee of Experts on Poverty, which is the one used by the DANE today, is taken into account, monetary poverty fell from 40.8% in 2012 to 34.7% in 2018, and extreme monetary poverty went from 11.7% in 2012 to 8.2% in 2018.

Regarding multidimensional poverty, the Colombian Multidimensional Poverty Index (C-MPI) dropped from 29.7% in 2010 to 19.1% in 2018, based on the updated methodology with 2018 census data, which is the one the DANE is using at the moment.

Regardless of the index used or the methodology applied, it is clear that Colombia experienced a positive social transformation in the 2010s: a 13-percentage-point decrease in monetary poverty and more than a 7-point decrease in extreme monetary poverty between 2009 and 2018 (according to the MESEP methodology) and more than a 10-percentage-point decrease in multidimensional poverty between 2010 and 2018.

Despite this important progress, at the end of 2018, there was still significant work to be done: according to the new methodology, just under 35 out of 100 Colombians still lived in conditions of monetary poverty.

In August 2018, there was a change in State leadership and, with it, a corresponding change in some policies and programs, in priorities and objectives, as is natural in every democracy. The new administration, led by a member of the political party that had torpedoed the peace process with

The Battle Against Poverty. Juan Manuel Santos, Oxford University Press. © Juan Manuel Santos (2023).
DOI: 10.1093/oso/9780192885234.003.0011

the Revolutionary Armed Forces of Colombia (FARC) and had opposed it blindly and relentlessly, slowed down the implementation of many points in the peace agreement, such as those related to comprehensive rural development and political reform. Likewise, it canceled or downplayed social programs that had greatly improved living conditions, such as "Ser Pilo Paga" ("Being Smart Pays Off"), the free housing program for the poorest, and Red Unidos, to name just a few examples. Adding to this, like all other nations on the planet, Colombia experienced the devastating tsunami of the COVID-19 pandemic beginning in early 2020. Beyond the health emergency, the pandemic paralyzed the economy and led to company closures and budget restrictions: the perfect recipe for unemployment and poverty to rise again.

Despite this, the setback wasn't as big as it could have been. Since 2021, both economic and social indicators have shown recovery. In large part, this is because—and here is a very important lesson for other nations— we ensured the continuity of the main social and reconciliation programs, shielding them from the changes produced by political, economic, or any other kind of circumstances.

Programs such as the comprehensive early childhood care program, "De Cero a Siempre" ("From Zero to Forever"); the conditional assistance program, Familias en Acción (Families in Action), to encourage children's school attendance and nutritional check-ups; and programs that help large swaths of the population across the country's territory access social benefits now that a peace agreement has been signed with the FARC were incorporated into the nation's laws and became State policies. Regardless of the incumbent government leader or their political slant, these programs have a secure place in the national budget and must be implemented. The importance of this legal establishment of social programs cannot be emphasized enough, not only for Colombia but also for any country.

Additionally, the C-MPI—this innovative measure born within the University of Oxford, which our country was a pioneer in adopting—continues to be an instrument of reference for new national development plans and the measurement of progress on the Sustainable Development Goals.

The Current Outlook

What is the situation today, as the COVID-19 pandemic that paralyzed the world in 2020 begins to move toward an endemic that we will have to live with in the long term? Unemployment, which closed at 9.7% in 2018, reached 13.7% in 2021 and 11.2% in 2022. In 2021, monetary poverty reached 39.3%, signifying an increase of 4.6 percentage points compared to the 2018 data.[1] Extreme monetary poverty also increased by four percentage points, rising from 8.2% in 2018 to 12.2% in 2021.[2]

In the face of these setbacks, which can be partly explained by the effects of the pandemic, there is an encouraging development. In 2021, the C-MPI stood at 16%, its lowest level since it began to be calculated in 2010. How can we understand a rise in monetary poverty but a drop in multidimensional poverty? I venture a hypothesis: pandemic-produced factors such as employment loss or the halt of informal activities resulted, obviously, in lower monetary incomes for Colombian families. Nevertheless, the achievements in increased coverage and quality in education, health, housing, utilities, connectivity, and other areas, which are the fruit of social policies and programs that have been implemented for at least a decade, have enabled improvements in several dimensions of poverty.[3]

We cannot forget that the C-MPI is valuable precisely because it serves as an extensive picture of the social situation. Not only does it show progress or setbacks, but it also signals where these take place. Although this national rate of 16% represents a step forward, the gap between urban and rural areas that the C-MPI reveals is concerning: while multidimensional poverty stood at 31.1% in rural areas, it stood at 11.5% in municipal seats, that is, in urban centers (*Portafolio*, 2022).

The inevitable conclusion is that much remains to be done. At the end of 2021, almost 4 out of every 10 Colombians—some 20 million people—were living in income poverty,[4] and 3 out of every 10 residents in the countryside were living in multidimensional poverty. The outlook continues to be challenging.

What Lies Ahead

In 2019 and 2021, Colombia experienced unprecedented marches and social protests. These cannot be attributed to the pandemic's effects since they began a year before it was declared. Moreover, the pandemic helped to calm down

---

[1] Percentages calculated by the DANE according to the methodology updated in 2020.
[2] Percentages calculated by the DANE according to the methodology updated in 2020.
[3] According to the director of the DANE at the time this data was released, the reduction in the C-MPI is mainly explained "by the significant improvement in living conditions for boys, girls, and young people in terms of school absenteeism" since school attendance rose by 10 percentage points from 2020 to 2021 (*El Tiempo*, 2022). However, many economists have questioned these numbers on school attendance due to a change in the way it is measured, even more so considering that in 2021 the COVID-19 pandemic restricted access to education not only in Colombia but also worldwide.
[4] Considering the DANE's monetary poverty data calculated with the methodology updated in 2020.

feelings when the entire population had to be confined in 2020 during a mandatory months-long quarantine. The truth is that the country's poor and the emerging middle class took to the streets to demand simple improvements in their quality of life, which the administration in office did not know how to understand or handle; it responded with repression rather than dialogue. A proposed tax reform that particularly taxed the middle class and maintained exemptions for large corporations was the spark that lit the fire. And this disagreement between society and the government has resulted in consequences we are just beginning to observe.

I write this epilogue at the end of January 2023, when the president who is replacing President Duque for the next four years—from August 2022 to August 2026—has been in office for less than six months. The votes couldn't be more telling, and they have been interpreted as the result of people's rejection of, and indignation against, a leader and a political class that didn't want, or couldn't, connect with people's realities and needs. In the first round of elections, on May 29, 2022, the candidate supported by the incumbent administration and by most of the country's political parties was defeated. Two populist candidates who represented a break with traditional politics were left on the ballot for the second round: on the one hand, Gustavo Petro, former guerrilla member, former congressman, and former mayor of Bogotá, who represents a left-wing populist stance, and on the other hand, Rodolfo Hernández, a 77-year-old outsider, businessman, millionaire, and former mayor of Bucaramanga, a medium-sized city in northeastern Colombia, who represents another kind of populism, one based on pragmatism and not on ideologies or programs.

For the first time in Colombian history, the presidential office was decided between two candidates who never served in traditional parties. Both appealed to the popular narrative of the fight against corruption and against poverty. Finally, in a close second-round vote on June 19, 2022, Gustavo Petro was elected president.

What lies ahead is unpredictable. I hope the current president and his government team, to fulfill their campaign promises, will take into account the path summarized in this book, in particular to ensure that the remaining 20 million poor people in the country improve their living conditions. I also hope they respect and continue down the path of reconciliation that the 2016 peace agreement opened. What President Petro announced in his first days in office, in terms of legislative initiatives he will promote in Congress and the appointment of some of his ministers, gives cause for hope. In his words, his aim is to finally implement the peace agreement, including all the social and equity-oriented components this entails, in addition to prioritizing the fight against poverty and hunger and defending the environment. Only the facts will show whether such noble aims, which I support, are coupled with the ingredients that can make them a reality: the ability to govern, common sense, leadership, and convening power.

I am convinced that the peace agreement contains many of the solutions to continue making progress on equity and social development. If Point 1 of the agreement, which addresses comprehensive rural reform, is implemented, we would be resolving a very important part of the problem we are experiencing as poverty, inequality, and violence are concentrated in the countryside. The same applies to Point 4 on the issue of illicit drugs. Implementing a comprehensive program for substituting illegal crops, rather than insisting on spraying them, in addition to doing away with prohibition—a bold and controversial, but necessary step—would open up an opportunity for progress and peace in areas that have been ruled by drug trafficking and violence for years.

Today, Colombia has the tools—the peace agreement, the Sustainable Development Goals, the C-MPI, the social programs made into State policies—and, if there is political will, if there is positive leadership, the nation can be united around solutions that benefit the most vulnerable.

Less than eight years remain before we will know whether Colombia was able to meet its targets of reducing multidimensional poverty to 8.4% and minimizing extreme poverty. The year 2030, the Sustainable Development Goals' finishing line, is just around the corner. With commitment, will, and innovative ideas, and prioritizing people's most pressing needs, we can move ever closer to a present of social justice, not only in Colombia but also in many nations around the world.

This book is a humble contribution in that direction.

References

El Tiempo. (2022). "Más de 971.000 personas salieron de la pobreza multidimensional en el 2021." April 29. https://www.eltiempo.com/economia/sectores/pobreza-multidimensional-cuantos-salieron-de-esta-condicion-en-el-2021-668428.

Portafolio. (2022). "La pobreza multidimensional en Colombia en 2021 cayó a 16%." April 29. https://www.portafolio.co/economia/en-vivo-pobreza-multidimensional-en-colombia-2021-564682.

Index